Real-Life
MATH
Problem Solving

by Mark Illingworth

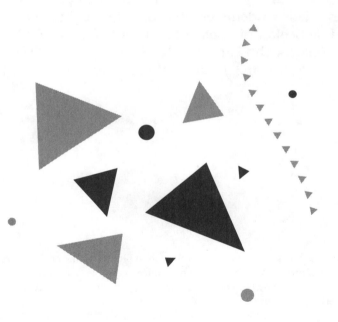

SCHOLASTIC
PROFESSIONAL BOOKS

New York • Toronto • London • Auckland • Sydney

This book is dedicated to Christa
McAuliffe and all teachers who, like
Christa, strive to be the best they can be
for their students.

Acknowledgments

This project was made possible by a grant from the Christa McAuliffe Sabbatical Trust Fund, a project of the New Hampshire Charitable Fund.

Thanks to my students, who have inspired me to develop these materials by sharing their imagination and enthusiasm. Thanks to Julie McCoy for guiding me with her insightful and invaluable suggestions, for moving my misplaced modifiers and unsplitting my infinitives, and for teaching me once and for all that exercise is not spelled with a "z." Finally, thanks to the following people who allowed me to work with them and their students or who shared thoughts, ideas, or materials that helped me improve this book: Fritz Bell, Marilyn Butler, Libby Collins, Paul Curtis, Anne Hoag, Karen Kelley, John Lamport, June Litwin, Cindy O'Leary, Jaylyn Olivo, Roger Parsons, Rachel Spaulding, Claire Watterson, and Randy Wormald.

Designed by Sydney Wright
Cover design by Vincent Ceci and Jaime Lucero
Cover illustrations by Hank Morehouse

Interior illustration by
ISBN: 0-590-48804-X
12 11 10 9 8 7   123/0

Contents

5—More Than Just Answers (Annotated Solutions)

Bibliography

Tools and Opportunities for
SOLVING
Complex Problems

DANCING, BASEBALL, AND MATH

Although you probably don't want to take a formal poll at your next social gathering, if you ask around you'll unfortunately find an abundance of adults who fear math or have a strong distaste for the subject.

Young children don't feel this way about math. First graders create patterns, add beans, and count blocks with the same open-minded enthusiasm with which they build cities in the sandbox or draw cubist murals with crayons. What happens to transform eager and confident young math students into quivering, digit-despising adolescents? Is there something inherently abhorrent about math? Or, as educators, do we fail to provide some important ingredient along the way that would help preserve our students' confidence

and interest in activities that involve math?

▲ The Missing Ingredient ▲

Dancing, baseball, and math all require learning a set of routines. Each type of dance, from ballet and the bossa nova to the twist and the tarantella, has its own set of steps. Baseball requires batting practice, infield practice, outfield practice, and a strong knowledge of the rules. Similarly, math students have steps they must learn, skills they must practice, and a set of rules they must follow. After memorizing basic math facts and mastering addition, subtraction, multiplication, and division, typical math students progress to learn more difficult operations with fractions, decimals, and percents. Finally, primed by these energizing topics, they eagerly take on algebra and other awe-inspiring high school math courses. Or do they?

The real joy of dance is the movement—the jumping, swinging, kicking, and swaying to music we enjoy. The thrill of baseball is the game—the feel of our cleats clawing dry dirt on the way to first as the voices of the crowd whip together into a unified, pulsing source of adrenaline. To make our math instruction meaningful, we must give our students the opportunity to "dance" in math. We need to give them mitts and then let them take the field.

We dance in math by solving real problems that stimulate us to generate ideas, collect and connect information, try out designs, invent, and use imagination and humor. For students, dancing in math might be climbing onto the floor with a ruler and a stopwatch to measure the speed of a battery-powered robot, using scale drawings to plan hamster condominiums, or optimizing a teddy bear assembly line to produce the most bears per day.

If we had spent 45-60 minutes per day for twelve years learning specific dance steps or practicing baseball skills, but rarely dancing or playing a game, how many of us would still enjoy these activities today? Similarly, we can't subject our students to twelve years of practicing math skills with only the promise that they'll need these skills someday. Like the architects, builders, carpenters, designers, accountants, clerks, engineers, and entrepreneurs they may someday become, students must be able to define, examine, diagnose, unravel, and explain real and complicated problems—and they can be led to experience this as an enjoyable process.

> "Students must be able to define, examine, diagnose, unravel, and explain real and complicated problems— and they can be led to experience this as an enjoyable process."

OTHER TECHNIQUES

▲ ▲ ▲ ▲ ▲ ▲ ▲ ▲ ▲ ▲ ▲ ▲ ▲ ▲

In other publications you'll find problems for teaching students how to look for a pattern, guess and check, use an easier example, work backwards, make a list or table, build a model, or draw a graph. These are all useful techniques. Many of them are embodied within or can be used to solve the problems in this book. In addition, you can use the general techniques you learn from this book to design your own units for teaching any of the problem-solving techniques listed above.

REAL-WORLD PROBLEM SOLVING

The term *problem solving* has become as commonplace in math books as the words *all-natural* on food products. Although these buzz words may be important marketing tools, they provide us with very little knowledge of what we're really getting from a product. To alleviate this lack of clarity, here is the definition of problem solving that is embodied by the problems of this book.

Problem solving takes place when students think flexibly, creatively, and analytically to define, examine, diagnose, and unravel complicated problems. Students' work, beginning with the gathering of information and ending with the communication of their ideas, may result in solutions, decisions, conclusions, plans, or designs.

In support of this definition, Chapters 3 and 4 present two different problem-solving techniques. The first technique uses drawings to show how something is put together, which helps us design, size parts, and list materials for a project. The second technique diagrams a wide variety of information to further our understanding of a problem's complexities.

▲ Real World vs. Traditional Problems ▲

The following chart outlines the difference between problems typically posed in textbooks and problems that people are likely to encounter in the real world. The problems in this book intentionally incorporate aspects of the latter.

Traditional Textbook Problems	Real-World Problems
Most problems require only one step.	Problems require more than one step.
Each problem requires only one type of computation algorithm (+, -, x, ÷, etc.)	Problems are complex and require different algorithms for different steps.
The problems are contrived so students already know exactly which procedure to follow.	Problems occur naturally in context, and people must decide what procedure or problem-solving techniques will help.
There is usually one correct solution.	There are often many viable solutions. Which solution is chosen generally depends on decisions and judgments made along the way.
All the data are provided.	Data are often missing or there are too many data. People must decide what data are needed and then research or measure to collect them.
Problems come out evenly.	Problems might have awkward answers, or sometimes a "good" solution is impossible.

AN UNLIKELY SCENARIO
▲▲▲▲▲▲▲▲▲▲▲▲▲▲

Mel works in the Marketing Department of the Mushie Tofu Company. One morning, just as Mel thought about the egg and quail sandwich he was going to have for lunch at the restaurant next door, his boss, Marilyn, walked into his office with a question. She said they sold 45 cases of tofu in the southern New Hampshire region during the last two weeks. She asked Mel to figure out how many cases they'd have to sell over the next two weeks if they were to sell a total of 100 cases for the month. Mel's face fell and his stomach objected as he realized he'd have to work right through lunch to solve this one.

AN PLAUSIBLE SCENARIO
▲▲▲▲▲▲▲▲▲▲▲▲▲▲

Mel works in the Marketing Department of the Mushie Tofu Company. One day last year, his boss, Marilyn, asked him to develop some new marketing strategies for the southern New Hampshire region. With two weeks to work on the problem, Mel had to access computer records on sales through various distributors to the different retail stores. He had to analyze the data to look for ineffective marketing channels and develop several proposals to restructure the company's sales network. He then presented the options to Marilyn and the other members of the Marketing Department, and together they made the necessary decisions and implemented their new plan.

SUPPORTING NCTM STANDARDS

The NCTM Standards advance an ideal of math education: *"We must go beyond how we were taught and teach how we wish we had been taught. We must bring to life a vision of what a mathematics classroom should be."* The following quotes portray the qualities we should look for as students interact in such a classroom.

1. ACTIVE PARTICIPATION: *"The role of the students is redirected from passive recipients to active participants, from isolated workers to team members, from listeners to investigators and reporters, and from timid followers to intrepid explorers and risk takers."*

2. REAL-WORLD CONNECTIONS: Students should become familiar with the ways in which mathematics plays a role in their society. *"A primary goal for the study of mathematics is to give children experiences that promote the ability to solve problems and that build mathematics from situations generated within the context of everyday experiences."*

3. REAL PROBLEMS: *"Real-world problems are not ready-made exercises with easily processed procedures and numbers. Situations that allow students to experience problems with "messy" numbers or too much or not enough information or that have multiple solutions, each with different consequences, will better prepare them to solve problems they are likely to encounter in their daily lives."*

4. GATHERING: Students should be able to use a variety of methods in gathering information needed to solve a problem.

5. REASONING: Students should be able to make conjectures, test their ideas, and build arguments. They should be able to make rational estimations, assumptions, and decisions in solving long problems.

6. COMMUNICATION: *"As students communicate their ideas, they learn to clarify, refine, and consolidate their thinking."* Discussing mathematical ideas and solutions is part of using math in real-world situations.

7. MAKING MISTAKES: Students should be allowed to make and learn from mistakes. They should be rewarded for their reasoning and process, not just for the correct answer.

8. SELF-CONFIDENCE: *"As a result of studying mathematics, students need to view themselves as capable of using their growing mathematical power to make sense of new problem situations in the world around them."*

WHEN TO TEACH PROBLEM SOLVING

Problem solving is an approach to math that should be woven into all other math topics. As a matter of fact, problem solving can be the focus of your year, with computation skills serving as tools. In real life, we identify a problem, and then we look for the tools that will help us to solve it. How many times have you gone to the garage, picked out a tool, and then looked for a problem to solve with that tool?

▲ Integrating Problem Solving with other Math Topics ▲

Your curriculum is already packed. *"When will I ever have time to teach problem solving?"* you ask. First, you may need to take another look at your curriculum. Has your school revised its curriculum to reflect the NCTM's shift in emphasis from computation to problem solving? This changing focus in math should move some outdated topics out of the way to make room for problem solving. Second, after your students practice specific problem-solving skills, you can begin to mix problem-solving opportunities with other math topics you must teach. The two examples below show how this can be done. These examples also show how problem solving can lead to the exploration of using computational skills as tools.

Example 1—Decimals: Ask students to calculate the cost of filling their family car's gas tank and the distance the car could travel with a full tank of gas.

The problem requires students to gather data and it also requires work with decimals. You can introduce this problem before students have done computation with decimals. Now they have a reason to learn these new skills.

COMPUTATION AT HOME
▲▲▲▲▲▲▲▲▲▲▲▲▲▲

Okay, students still have to practice computation skills. But does this practice have to take up a lot of instructional time? Here's a way to give yourself more instructional time devoted to problem solving and projects.

Introduce a computational skill to the whole class, and then check students' understanding with practice problems or a pre-test. Those few students who still need help can meet with you briefly while the rest of the class works on problem solving projects. The class still has to increase their proficiency and speed with these new skills, but they can practice on homework assignments.

EMPOWER STUDENTS
▲▲▲▲▲▲▲▲▲▲▲▲▲▲

Teaching strategies for solving problems empowers students to approach and tackle a variety of challenges with confidence. As they are presented with more opportunities to use these strategies, their skills will become more valuable.

Lead your students to go beyond the problems in this book to maximize what they learn. Read the extensions that go along with each solution. Learn how to change sections of problems to create new problems. Let your students make up problems. Read the sections that describe how to integrate the techniques into other math topics. Invite students and guest speakers to share how they've used the techniques.

Example 2—Percents: A student is trying to earn $120 for a summer camp she'd like to attend. She convinces a local bike shop owner to give her a 15% commission on new bikes she sells outside of the store. How many $200 bicycles will she need to sell outside of the store?

15% means 15 out of every 100

| 100 ➡ 15 | 100 ➡ 15 | 100 ➡ 15 |

Students can apply diagrams to help solve this problem. Diagramming is the problem-solving technique presented in Chapter 4. (See the problem on page 61.) While teaching this problem-solving technique, you are also introducing percents.

SETTING THE TONE

The first week of the school year is the time to establish a mood of problem solving within your classroom. Math in the real world focuses on solving problems, not performing pencil and paper calculations. What are the types of problems students will be asked to solve in their jobs? How do mathematical expectations in careers differ from arithmetic? An introduction to problem solving at the beginning of the year should include answers to these questions.

▲ What Do People *Really* Do? ▲

Divide students into small groups and ask them to brainstorm to list careers and problems that might have to be solved in those jobs. Here are some examples:

Occupation: Painter/Decorator

Problem: A potential client has asked you to give her an estimate on painting and wallpapering several rooms in her home. She wants the work done by a specific date. How many people will you need on your crew? How much will supplies cost? How many hours will the job take? How much should you charge?

HELP FROM THE MEDIA
▲▲▲▲▲▲▲▲▲▲▲▲▲▲

The annotated bibliography describes two public television shows that inspire students by showing how math is used in a variety of careers. You can keep an eye out for these shows in the fall or write to the addresses provided to obtain the video cassettes. These shows are a great way to set the tone at the beginning of the year.

Occupation:	Bike Designer

Problem: Your company is trying to design a top-of-the-line bike that is four ounces lighter than the bikes of your competitors. How can you change the tubing size and shape to achieve this weight loss without sacrificing strength?

Have each group list ten occupation-related problems and then select their favorite to present to the rest of the class.

▲ Inventions are the Result of Solved Problems ▲

Assign each group of students an invention and ask them to list 20-30 problems that had to be solved in order for that invention to exist. The list may require some research. Here are problems that had to be solved regarding light bulbs:

- How thick should the glass be?

- How thick should the tungsten wire be so that it doesn't burn out too quickly?

- How long should the tungsten wire be so that the right amount of electricity flows through it?

- How can these light bulbs be manufactured easily?

A CHALLENGE FOR YOU
▲▲▲▲▲▲▲▲▲▲▲▲▲▲

Viewing the world in the context of problems with solutions may be a new way of thinking for you. Don't feel like you have to know all the answers; it's more important that you're able to ask the questions.

On your way home from school, view things you see as a result of problem solving or as the source of a new problem. See if you can identify at least ten problems or solved problems by the time you get home.

Conducting a
PROBLEM-
SOLVING
Classroom

TIPS FOR GUIDING PROBLEM SOLVERS

▲ Setting the Mood and Modeling an Approach ▲

1. There's always more than one way to solve a problem. Create an environment where students are encouraged to find their own methods and individuality in reasoning is welcomed.

2. As you help individuals, resist the temptation to move them in the direction of *your* solution, no matter how incredibly elegant and sophisticated it might be. It is important to give students the opportunity to grow by finding their own solutions. When the class is sharing solutions, by all means share

yours, but remember to present it as another alternative, not as the best way.

3. If there is an equation or simple procedure that would solve a problem or part of a problem instantly, you are helping a student by *withholding* this inside information. Students will grow through their own explorations, and their discoveries will provide a background that will help them understand short-cuts later.

4. When students are stuck, ask questions that will lead them just to the next stepping stone of understanding. Providing enough information to move students along without giving away too much of the solution is an art. Samples of leading questions are provided later in this chapter and with each solution page in Chapter 5.

5. As you check in with students about their work, praise them for their process. What you choose to compliment will influence what they view as important. Point out how well they have gathered information or organized their steps. Notice clever or unusual problem-solving methods. Compliment them as they try something new, even when they're stuck.

6. Avoid simply telling students that their answers are correct. When students finish problems, they immediately want to know if they're correct. By responding too quickly, we cheat them out of an opportunity to build trust in their own work, and we place the emphasis on the correct answer rather than the process. Instead, respond by asking them to explain the steps they followed. Point out the reasonableness in these steps. Ask them if the steps make sense to them and, at the end, ask them whether *they* think their solutions are right or not.

7. Give students a chance to communicate their solutions to you verbally, even if you know that they've done it right. Sharing the reasoning behind a solution is a skill that is part of mathematics in the real world, and students need opportunities to practice. Also, this is a perfect time for you to compliment the process.

8. Your evaluation system should emphasize the process that students have followed, although it can also include a check of the final answer. By placing the weight of your evaluation on *how* the students worked, you make a strong statement about what you feel is most important. Evaluation forms are provided with each of the problem-solving techniques presented in Chapters 3 and 4.

▲ Noticing & Responding to Students' Work Habits ▲

9. Emphasize neatness. Preparing a neat presentation demands an organized thinking process and minimizes calculation errors. Also, learning to communicate solutions clearly in writing is a skill that is part of using math in real-world tasks.

10. Notice the readability of students' work. Some may have developed a writing style appropriate for microfiche. Often this is not a problem, but sometimes it can result in errors. Encourage students to work large scale when they are doing drawings and diagrams. A larger scale leaves room to add detail and communicates more effectively to others who are trying to read the work.

11. Always encourage students to take a first step. Many students will wait a long time before putting anything down on paper. Problems can look foreboding and impossible to solve at first glance, but initial steps often lead the way to new insights. In problem solving, the first steps are to read the problem and collect information that may help to solve it. Tell students that your offer to help becomes effective after they have done at least these two steps.

12. Let students use calculators. They are tools, just as word processors are tools for writing. Asking students to do all the calculations by hand will misdirect their energies and may discourage some students. The NCTM Standards encourage the use of calculators; if we are trying to emulate real-world problem solving, then calculators and/or computers are clearly appropriate tools.

▲ Managing the Work Sessions ▲

13. Provide time for quiet study *and* for shared study. As will be discussed later in this chapter *(Learning Styles & Individual Tastes)*, some students prefer each of these work atmospheres. Although students should have opportunities to work in their preferred styles, they also benefit from participating in the opposite style.

14. Provide an area in your room where pairs of students can confer, even during a quiet work time. To make this experience most effective, you'll have to model how to share ideas without just giving away answers.

15. Allow students to work alone if this is their preference, even when others are working in groups. Although asking these students to spend *some* time in groups is appropriate to their development, the desire to work independently stems from what is most comfortable or effective for them, not from a shortcoming that needs to be corrected.

16. Encourage individual expression. Some students may choose to add details, designs, or drawings to the problems, or they may make up their own versions. By sharing this part of their personalities, they are telling you they have found a way to make the work even more fun for themselves. Capitalize on this expression.

ORGANIZING THE CLASS

This section shows you how to make room for problem-solving within your school schedule, how to set up your classroom, and how to plan a problem-solving unit.

▲ Planning Your Schedule ▲

If you're not sure how you're going to make time for a problem-solving unit within your packed curriculum, the first thing to do is to see whether your school's curriculum reflects the same problem-solving emphasis as the NCTM Standards. (See pages 8 and 9.) Then look for opportunities to integrate topics you need to teach with problems from this book or with other projects. List the topics you're supposed to cover during the year. The example below shows a portion of a typical sixth grade curriculum.

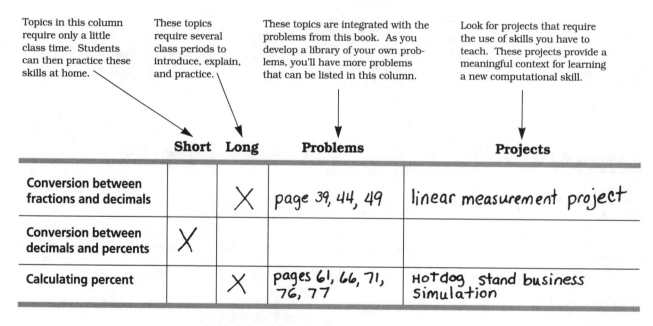

Topics in this column require only a little class time. Students can then practice these skills at home.

These topics require several class periods to introduce, explain, and practice.

These topics are integrated with the problems from this book. As you develop a library of your own problems, you'll have more problems that can be listed in this column.

Look for projects that require the use of skills you have to teach. These projects provide a meaningful context for learning a new computational skill.

	Short	Long	Problems	Projects
Conversion between fractions and decimals		X	page 39, 44, 49	linear measurement project
Conversion between decimals and percents	X			
Calculating percent		X	pages 61, 66, 71, 76, 77	Hotdog stand business simulation

Table 2.1—A Cross-Reference to the Curriculum

Once you've listed the topics, problem-solving units, and projects you'd like to teach, you can begin mapping out your year. Use the two right-hand columns in Table 2.1 as a guide for teaching new concepts through problem solving or projects. Table 2.2 is a teacher's plan for the beginning of the school year. Notice that basic skills are introduced in class and then practiced at home, leaving class instructional time for the development of problem-solving skills.

WEEK OF	IN CLASS	AT HOME
9/1	1. Review mult. of 3-dig. by 2-dig. numbers 2. Intro. to problem solving (see *Setting the Tone*, page 10)	Practice multiplication to build speed
9/8	1. Review division with 2-digit divisors 2. Begin prob-solving unit (Technique A Chapter 3)	Practice multiplication and division
9/15	Continue prob-solving unit teaching the use of drawings to solve problems. (Introduce new topics as they arise in the problem.)	Practice multiplication and division
9/22		Complete home project from Chapter 3
	New unit, etc.	

Table 2.2—Mapping Out the School Year

▲ The Classroom ▲

Here are several features you should include in your problem-solving classroom:

1. Set up a material center that includes, rulers, tape measures, yardsticks, meter sticks, stopwatches, scales, balances, and containers for measuring volume. Provide materials such as toothpicks, cubes, and tiles that students can use for modeling problems.

2. Use room dividers, bookshelves, or furniture to establish at least one conference area where a pair of students can go during quiet work times to talk about a problem.

3. Designate large areas of the walls for displays of students' work and *Spice It Up* creations. The students need plenty of opportunities to share what they produce, both to build self-esteem and to practice communication of mathematical solutions. (See *The Math Art Gallery*, right.)

4. Set up an area where you can post challenge problems and where students can display problems they've made up for their classmates.

5. Build a library of puzzle books and books that describe applications of math. Occasionally take time to describe one of these books.

▲ Presenting a Problem-Solving Unit ▲

Figures 2.3 and 2.4 show two day-by-day plans for presenting a problem-solving unit. Both of these plans (or any plan that you devise) should include the following features:

1. In order to learn any of the three problem-solving techniques in this book, students should work through six to twelve problems.

2. Students should have some choices about which problems they work on at specific times. They should enjoy the same autonomy over their work that we enjoy when we make choices about the pacing and the order in which we complete our tasks. The plans provided show how this latitude can be achieved within a highly-structured unit.

3. Students should also have choices about which of their solutions are used as evaluation tools. Although the students should always be held accountable for quality work, the pressure of a formal evaluation can stifle their explorations of new ideas encountered while solving a problem.

4. Students need opportunities to share their ideas and solutions in small and large groups.

5. Students need opportunities to practice communicating mathematically—both orally and in writing.

6. Students should be encouraged to exercise their own creativity, imagination, and humor through some of the *Spice It Up* activities. (See page 20.)

THE MATH ART GALLERY
▲▲▲▲▲▲▲▲▲▲▲▲▲▲▲▲▲

Foster an environment where students take pride in producing a well-thought out, well-constructed, and nicely displayed solution. Each solution should begin with a listing of the facts needed to solve the problem, followed by a step-by-step explanation with all quantities clearly labeled.

Talk about the importance of presentation when trying to obtain a job or a promotion. An organized presentation often wins over colleagues or clients. Set up an art gallery in your class or school and invite parents and other classes to see it. Any problem from this book could result in displays, models, or presentations.

WHERE'S THE TEACHER?
▲▲▲▲▲▲▲▲▲▲▲▲▲▲▲▲▲

While your students are working on problems alone or in pairs, your job is to interact with them as much as possible. Offer help as needed, but also invite students to share with you. Ask them to explain their reasoning, even though what they've done is clear to you. Compliment their ideas, insights, and work habits. Ask "What if?" questions to check or deepen their understanding. This is your chance to share your enthusiasm, observe how your students learn, and make your students feel good about themselves.

7. Students should sometimes work alone and sometimes work with one or two classmates.

Each of the day-to-day plans below is based on a problem-solving unit requiring the solution of ten problems. The length of time required for such a unit ranges from two to four weeks. You'll be able to gauge the time required by your students after you've had more experience leading them through these problems.

Table 2.3—Two Problems at a Time

Day 1
• Demonstrate the problem-solving technique with several problems. Demonstrate how to collect relevant facts and work in organized steps.
• Give students a contract listing work that they'll need to complete. (See sample in Chapter 3.)
• Assign partners.
• Assign computation practice that students will complete at home.

Days 2–3
• Begin each day with a 2-minute check-in. Each pair of students tells you what they're working on that day.
• Work on two problems from the assigned set.
• Assign one pair of students to lead the solution discussion on Day 4.
• Students who finish early may preview other problems, work on problem extensions, challenge problems posted in the room, or complete *Spice It Up* activities.

Day 4
• One student pair presents their solution and conducts a discussion to share different solution methods.
• Present problem extensions and variations.
• Invite students to share and then display *Spice It Up* creations.
• Collect solutions that students have chosen to be formally evaluated by you.

Days 5–15
• Repeat the pattern of Days 2-4.
• Assign the home project (see page 32) one or two weeks before the end of the unit.

Table 2.4—Students Pace Themselves

Day 1
• The first day is the same as in the unit plan to the left.

Day 2
• Students work problems in any order.
• Give students a schedule to show when various problems will be discussed in class. They must have those problems completed before the discussion dates. Assign a pair of students to lead each of the scheduled discussions.
• Begin each day with a 2-minute check-in. Each pair of students tells you what they're working on that day.

Days 3–15
• Students work on problems in any order they choose, but they must have problems completed according to the discussion schedule.
• In order to meet their contracts, students must complete a certain number of problems and *Spice It Up* activities.
• During discussions, share solution variations and present problem extensions.
• Students continue practicing computational skills at home.
• Assign the home project (see page 32) one or two weeks before the end of the unit.
• According to the contract, students will submit some solutions for formal evaluation and some for a quick overview. Evaluate solutions as you go along rather than collecting them at the end of the unit. Students will improve their performance on problems as they learn what attributes you're looking for in their work.

LEARNING STYLES & INDIVIDUAL TASTES

The students in your math class each have their own preferred work styles. Many systems have been developed for classifying individual personality traits and learning styles. Familiarity with these schemes will prepare you to set up your classroom to meet a wide range of student needs and preferences.

▲ Introverts & Extroverts ▲

The Myers-Briggs Type Classification system consists of four categories that reflect how people gather and process information and interact with other people and their environment. In each category, individuals show a preference toward one of two styles, varying in degree from person to person along a continuum. The annotated bibliography recommends several resources for learning about this classification system.

One of the categories focuses on how often people like to think out loud with others. Extroverted students (70% of the population) need opportunities to talk out problems with others because this communication moves along their thinking. They are fueled by exchanging ideas and like to work in groups. Introverted students (30% of the population) may seem to take a long time to start a problem and they prefer to work alone or with only one partner. They dislike interruptions, and other people's thinking out loud can break their chain of thought.

Here are two suggestions for accommodating the needs of introverted and extroverted students: (1) Have *all* students start a problem on their own. Give them five to ten minutes to read and understand a problem and collect the necessary facts. After students have had this opportunity for independent thought, they can begin working with their partners. (2) Assign some problems to be completed together and some problems to be completed independently.

▲ Balancing the Hemispheres ▲

Just as they have a preferred learning style, students are usually stronger in thinking with either the right or the left hemisphere of the brain. We can make problem solving more universally appealing and make the learning experience more memorable to all students by putting both hemispheres to work.

INDEPENDENCE IS OKAY

Cooperative groups are a welcome addition to our teaching repertoire. Group work addresses the needs of the large percentage of the student population that works and thinks better with others. Be careful, however, not to compel *all* students to work in pairs or groups all of the time.

A student who expresses a preference for working alone is merely telling you that this is how he or she thinks best. Be flexible. Encourage students to develop skills in working cooperatively, but sometimes give students the option of working by themselves.

TWO IMPORTANT HALVES

Important discoveries and creative breakthroughs are usually achieved by systematic and analytic work, followed by an intuitive or insightful leap. One side of the brain can't do it all alone.

Type-Stereotypes

▲ ▲ ▲ ▲ ▲ ▲ ▲ ▲ ▲ ▲ ▲ ▲ ▲ ▲ ▲ ▲

In large part, school mathematics and training for the sciences typically tax the left brain more than the right. As a result, people who tend to succeed in math and science are often strong at analyzing. This situation sometimes leads to uncomplimentary and deceptive stereotyping of science and math people as individuals who analyze well but who are lacking in artistic, creative, or social gifts.

On the other hand, people with a right-brain dominance are often portrayed as being "artsy." Neither stereotype is valid; one strong hemisphere does not preclude another strong hemisphere. This false dichotomy should be dismissed, as it unjustly makes some careers seem unappealing or even foreboding to young people.

Two-Brained Careers

▲ ▲ ▲ ▲ ▲ ▲ ▲ ▲ ▲ ▲ ▲ ▲ ▲ ▲ ▲ ▲

Many careers use both sides of the brain. Product designs are the result of brainstorming, many stages of creativity, and attention to aesthetics, but they are also the result of analytical work to identify market demands, make financial plans, and build and test prototypes. Providing services or entertainment, running programs, and marketing goods require a combination of generating ideas and then doing the legwork.I

We use the left brain to separate and analyze parts, and the right brain to see things as a whole. Our left brain helps us process information linearly, one step at a time, a process used for encoding and decoding language and for logical analysis of problems. The right brain, by processing information in parallel, enables us to recognize relationships and make connections among parts or between dissimilar topics, leading to insight and creativity.

Mathematics, as we have traditionally learned it, is a predominantly left-brain endeavor. Our place value system, arithmetic, and simple word problems can be understood and handled by the sequential left hemisphere of our brains. But what about our right hemisphere? The complications of the problems in Chapters 3 and 4 draw upon the talents of both sides of the brain. The right brain is responsible for making connections, identifying patterns, representing information symbolically, and thinking divergently to gather information that might be relevant to the problem. The left brain, with its talent for clear analysis, follows up in processing any leads that were generated by the right brain.

▲ Spice It Up ▲

Imagination and humor have been incorporated into the problems in this book because the author likes exercising his right brain and because these qualities help students see how the context for problems can be richer than what they expect. The activities in the *Spice It Up* section of each problem invite students to use *their* imaginations and senses of humor to create a finished product that is more than a numerical value. Use *Spice It Up* activities as a part of the regular diet in your classroom, not as an occasional filler. By giving students opportunities to use their right brains to create, you'll make your math classroom an inviting place for a wider variety of students.

ASKING LEADING QUESTIONS

Naturally, as teachers, we all want our students to understand and succeed. However, our desire to achieve this goal can sometimes lead us astray from what is really best for students; they need opportunities to grow through the process of overcoming difficulties.

In our efforts to impart understanding, we sometimes divulge too much information. We don't want students to be desperately stuck or inconsolably frustrated, but we do want them to rely on their own resources, thinking, and perseverance. Carefully chosen but subtle comments and questions can lead students to develop their own thoughtful strategies and feel confident in their abilities to untie knotted problems on their own. Offering students just enough help to move them to the next level of understanding without giving them too much of the answer is a skill that you can develop with practice.

▲ Drawing Upon What Students Already Know ▲

1. If a student is stuck but hasn't formulated a specific question, ask him or her to show you what he or she has already done. The explanation will help you check the accuracy of the interpretation of the problem and will show you more specifically where and why he or she is stuck.

The student will often gain a more clear understanding of a problem simply by explaining the work to you; sometimes he or she will even be able to figure out what to do without your help.

Teacher: *Can you tell me what your goal is in solving this problem? It looks as if you've already written something down. Can you show me what you've tried so far?*

2. Students often assume a passive role when receiving help. If your knowledge of a student's abilities and your discussion about a problem lead you to suspect he or she is not fully applying himself or herself to the solution, reverse roles. Ask the student to become the teacher, and ask her or him to explain the problem to you. You may be surprised at how resourceful he or she becomes in solving the problem. However, no harm is done if the student is still stuck; you can try another technique.

ASKING OR TELLING
▲ ▲ ▲ ▲ ▲ ▲ ▲ ▲ ▲ ▲ ▲ ▲ ▲ ▲

When you prompt students, they'll look at you with questioning eyes as they respond with answers. For example, if you ask a student what the area of a 3-in. by 4-in. rectangle is, he or she may say 12 square inches, but the eyes and tone of voice will be imploring you to say if the answer is correct. Don't supply immediate gratification.

In reply to these requests for validation, try saying, "Are you asking me or telling me 12 square inches?" Your restraint will force students to develop a sense of confidence in their own answers.

DO YOUR HOMEWORK
▲ ▲ ▲ ▲ ▲ ▲ ▲ ▲ ▲ ▲ ▲ ▲ ▲ ▲

As you circulate through the classroom and talk with students who have requested assistance, you'll quickly realize how important it is to have a thorough understanding of the assigned problems. Being prepared is especially crucial if students are working on different problems because you'll have to shift gears quickly as you move from one student to the next.

The best way to prepare yourself to help students is to try the problems yourself so you can experience the reasoning involved and foresee the pitfalls. After solving the problems yourself, review the annotated solutions in this book, which explain several ways of approaching each problem and provide additional information that may strengthen your discussions with students.

Teacher: *Let's try something different. You're now the teacher and I'm your student. I don't get it. How do I know whether to multiply or divide here? Pictures sometimes help me understand. Could you draw me a picture? What's that thingamabob in the corner?*

3. Ask students to include units in their explanations. Students make many errors because they lose track of whether they're talking about inches or feet, grams or kilograms, or frogs or snakes.

Teacher: *So, you got 69 when you multiplied those two numbers together. Do you mean 69 bald zebras, 69 licorice whips, 69 inches, or 69 gerbil toes? 69 what? Are you sure you mean inches and not square inches? Explain.*

▲ One Step at a Time ▲

4. Many students may be stuck because their experiences are predominantly with shorter problems in which the solution is immediately apparent. These students will need to break the problem into parts.

Teacher: *Your description of the problem sounds pretty complete. I think you're stuck because you're used to solving the whole problem in your head before putting anything down on paper. I recommend that you try solving this problem in pieces. Instead of covering the whole wall with records at once, can you show me one small area of the room that you can figure out easily?*

5. Students should begin all problems by gathering and listing relevant facts. These facts are an excellent reference for solving a problem in steps. Show students how individual facts can be applied one at a time until the path to a solution becomes clear.

Teacher: *What does the first fact tell you about the distance between the two stores? Draw that for me, please. Good, now use the information from the second fact to add a detail to your drawing.*

6. Once a student has completed a solution in clearly defined steps, you can suggest that he or she check specific steps again if you see a mistake. This suggestion will minimize frustration by making it clear that she or he doesn't have to start from the beginning, but also because it will preserve self-esteem by showing that many steps are correct.

Teacher: *What you've done so far is great, and I think you're almost done with this problem. I can see one detail you've overlooked. Maybe you can check this third step one more time. Which facts did you use for this step? Does your work agree with that fact?*

▲ A Sampling of Techniques for Offering Help ▲

7. Use simpler examples. Suppose a problem calls for covering the floor of a 12-ft x 15-ft room with 9-in. square tiles. A student has converted the dimensions of the room to inches but doesn't see what to do next. An example with smaller numbers may help this student to better visualize the quantitative relationships involved.

Teacher: *Look at this smaller room. You'd have to be a pretty small person to live in it because it's only 18 inches wide by 27 inches long. How many of these tiles would it take to cover the floor of this room? How did you figure that out so fast? What do you mean? You multiplied? Explain. Will this technique work in the larger room?*

8. Your students should have access to cubes, square tiles, beans, and other manipulative materials they can use to model problems. Demonstrate the use of these materials as you help them individually.

Teacher: *Let this yellow bar stand for the distance the jet-powered skateboard travels in 1 hour. How long is this yellow bar? Right. Now, use more of these yellow bars to show how far the skateboard travels in 3 hours. How far is that? How did you figure that out?*

9. Ask students to clarify their understanding of problems by acting them out.

Teacher: *Let's put your chair on this green paper. Pretend this chair is your spaceship and this green paper is Earth. Where are you going? Pick a point in the room to represent the moon. What's going to happen to you on the way to the moon? Right. Start moving towards the moon, and tell me when you're at the spot where you run out of fuel.*

10. Avoid preconceived ideas about how a problem "should" be solved; your expectations may block you from finding an alternative, more suitable way to help a student. Consider a problem in which students must find the number of boxes needed to hold 420 cupcakes. One student has found that a box holds 70 cupcakes, but, despite your expert assis-

HOW NOT TO FIGHT
▲▲▲▲▲▲▲▲▲▲▲▲▲▲

Occasionally you will encounter students who have interpreted problems in what seem to be incorrect ways. Here are some suggestions for avoiding confrontations.

1. Give the student an opportunity to explain his or her reasoning without interruptions.

2. If the student's interpretation is at all reasonable and the accompanying solution is consistent with this interpretation, acknowledge that you can see how the problem could be interpreted and solved that way.

3. Discuss the problem and your interpretation, but let go of the need to have him or her acknowledge your interpretation as the best.

4. In deciding how to score a solution, ask yourself the following questions: (1) Did the student reason through the interpretation before he or she did the problem, or is the student coming up with an explanation simply to justify the answer? (2) Should I give full or partial credit for the student's solution, or should I ask her or him to rework the problem with the expected interpretation?

tance, he cannot see that 420 must be divided by 70. Although you'd like him to see the more sophisticated division relationship, the goal is to help him find a solution that he understands and feels confident about using.

Teacher: *Draw a box. How many cupcakes does that box hold? Why don't you write "70" right on the box? Now, add a second box. How many cupcakes will those two boxes hold? Good. Try adding a third box. How many cupcakes will those boxes hold? If you keep adding boxes, how will you know when you have enough? How many boxes do you think it will take?*

11. When you make a direct suggestion to a student about a technique phrase it as a question.

Teacher (the directive suggestion): *Let each mark on this ruler stand for a foot, and make a scale drawing of the doghouse.*

Teacher (the question): *The doghouse is too big to draw on your paper, but can you think of a way to use this ruler to draw a smaller version of each side of the doghouse?*

12. Don't hover. Give encouragement and a bit of help, but when the student is ready, go away and check in again later. Other students are waiting for your help, and sometimes you'll be surprised at what students can accomplish when they're nudged towards independence.

Teacher: *I don't want to give you any more hints because I think you understand the problem. I'm going to let you work on this step for awhile. I'll come back later to see how you're doing.*

▲ Boosting Self-Esteem ▲

13. You have opportunities to compliment students on what they have done well every time you visit their desks. Look for parts of solutions that are accurate, complete, or neatly presented, have interesting details, or show keen insight. Build confidence with concrete feedback; then guide students forward.

Teacher: *I love all the detail you're putting into your drawing. Not only does it clearly explain the problem, but your little cartoon ducks make it fun. So what is your question?*

HELP STUDENTS TO HELP STUDENTS

As described in *Organizing the Class* , make some provision for students to discuss problems and help each other. If left to their own methods, most students will give answers because it's the most obvious way to help.

If you want your students to help each other in a less directive way, you'll need to model this skill. Conduct demonstration "help" sessions with student volunteers. Allow the class to observe these sessions, and then discuss what they noticed about the way you asked questions. As the year progresses, ask pairs of student volunteers to conduct demonstration conferences with each other. Check in on student conferences periodically to learn how well your students are applying the techniques you have demonstrated.

14. You may spot a glaring inconsistency between the facts and what a student has done. Ask questions that lead the student to spot the error on his or her own.

Teacher: *Your diagram shows 4 ducks for every 3 hogs. How did you know how many of each to draw? Which fact told you that? Could you show me?*

15. When you discover an answer that lacks common sense, resist the temptation to point out the error directly or laugh. Instead, repeat the answer back to the student. Usually, the student will catch the mistake on his or her own. The goal is to preserve self-esteem and to nurture confidence.

Teacher: *So, your answer is that each truck will carry 10.5 sheep?* (If that doesn't work, try again.) *Does the number of sheep seem odd to you?*

SELF-ESTEEM
▲ ▲ ▲ ▲ ▲ ▲ ▲ ▲ ▲ ▲ ▲ ▲ ▲ ▲

The NCTM Standards suggest that students' evaluations affect their feelings about themselves: "An exclusive reliance on a single type of assignment can frustrate students, diminish their self-confidence, and make them feel anxious about or antagonistic towards mathematics."

Just as we cater to individual learning styles, we should provide a variety of ways in which students can demonstrate and use their knowledge, making it possible for each to find a way to be successful.

ASSESSING STUDENTS' WORK

To meaningfully and fairly evaluate students in math, we need to look at many aspects of their work. A little league coach is a poor coach indeed if he or she only looks at the final score of the game. The best coaches watch their players closely to learn how they can help them improve and capitalize on opportunities to praise accomplishments.

As students solve the problems in this book, we, as math coaches, must help them become aware of what they do well and of how they can improve. We need to take a broad view of our math students, a view that encompasses how they think and work as well as the solutions they arrive at. Each of the problem-solving sets in Chapters 3 and 4 includes an evaluation sheet that rewards each student for completeness in gathering data, skill in applying techniques, the step-by-step organization of a solution, and the reasonableness of the final solution. We must also give honest praise for these same qualities in their work whenever possible.

As you interact with students as they solve problems, you'll be better prepared to improve your own instruction and to help your students chart their course toward improvement. The following chart can be used as part of a portfolio evaluation or as a guide.

 ## Problem-Solving Portfolio

▶ *Observations of Work Styles, Strengths, and Attitudes*

The following key is used to comment on the student's strengths, attitudes, and work styles. Please understand that the goal is to comment on those areas that pertain to the individual student's work, not to put a mark, comment, or score next to *each* item on the list.

!!! = This is a strength for the student! He or she does this very well.
G = This would provide a good goal. She or he should work towards growth in this area.
O = The student does this often.
S = The student does this sometimes.

Methods & Work Style

___1. The student interprets problems thoroughly before proceeding to solve them.
___2. The student efficiently gathers the facts needed to solve the problems.
___3. The student misinterprets or reasons erroneously by taking short-cuts.
___4. The student makes use of the technique being taught.
___5. The student shows flexibility in drawing upon other techniques.
___6. The student focuses on just one way to solve a problem and gets "stuck."
___7. The student thinks about answers to make sure they are sensible.
___8. The student estimates to check answers.
___9. The student takes pride in the final presentation of solutions.

When Stuck, the Student...

___1. rereads the problem to gain clarity or to notice details previously overlooked.
___2. reviews the steps of what he or she has done so far to make sure it makes sense and finds new insights.
___3. experiments with a variety of techniques.
___4. goes on to another problem.
___5. gets VERY frustrated with himself/herself.
___6. loses confidence and/or concentration.
___7. seeks help, not answers, from others.
___8. uses time inappropriately.

In Reasoning, the Student....

___1. thinks logically and progressively.
___2. pursues several ideas at once.
___3. sees patterns and connections.
___4. draws unsupported conclusions.
___5. focuses on an idea and carries it through.
___6. abandons ideas too quickly.

In Communicating, the Student....

___1. explains clearly and effectively in written solutions.
___2. gives sequential explanations of his or her reasoning.
___3. gives explanations that jump back and forth between parts, but show understanding of the problem.
___4. helps other students understand problems without giving the answers.

Interest and More

___1. The student eagerly goes after challenges.
___2. The student's interest depends greatly on his or her mood of the day.
___3. The student experiments or creates new problems by asking "What if?"
___4. The student makes connections between problems and other applications.

The Student's Confidence Is....

___1. low, but he or she forges ahead.
___2. low, and this affects how she or he works.
___3. average, and he or she sometimes likes difficult problems.
___4. average, but she or he is intimidated by difficult problems.
___5. high, and he or she enjoys new challenges.

Notes

Show How It's

PUT TOGETHER

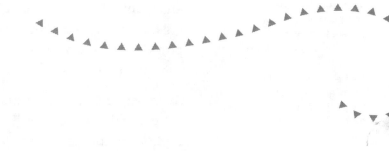

WHAT'S THE BIG IDEA?

During the process of design, building, or assembly, questions and problems often arise that can be clarified and solved more easily if we can see what things look like. Drawings offer new insights by showing how pieces fit together; by helping us to plan the shapes and sizes of individual parts; by pointing out what materials we'll need and how each should be cut or shaped; and by giving us a preview of how a design will look. Making clear drawings is a skill that can move us ahead on a variety of problems when we're stuck.

Architects, drafters, fashion designers, costumers, mechanics, electricians, tailors, decorators, carpenters, contractors, navigators, engineers, landscapers, and city planners are some of the professionals who sometime use drawings. In our personal lives, all of us may find drawings useful when adding to a home, remodeling, redecorating, or planning where the furniture will go. Drawings often are useful with our hobbies—such as building, sewing, painting, or gluing.

PRESENTING THIS TECHNIQUE

Before you introduce the problems (they begin on page 34) to your students, review the general tips for conducting a problem-solving classroom in Chapter 2. (Solutions to Technique A problems are found on pages 85 –87.)

▲ Getting Started ▲

1. Choose 8-12 problems from this chapter that you plan to have students solve. (Ideally, teachers in two or three grade levels will share problems so that students develop skills over several years.)

2. Read the annotated solutions found in Chapter 5 to the problems you plan to present. These solutions will give you an idea of what an organized solution might look like, so you can model this organization for students. The annotations will also provide a variety of methods that students might use to solve the problems.

3. Prepare a contract for students that lists the problems they'll solve and the points they'll receive for various components of this unit. A sample contract is provided on page 30.

4. Ask your students to brainstorm to list situations in which a drawing would be used to solve a problem.

5. Guide your class through the solution of several sample problems. (Three demonstration problems are provided below.) As you demonstrate, model collecting the facts and working in a step-by-step fashion. Students should begin to develop a methodical approach to unraveling problems, such as the six-step process shown.

6. Have students begin working on problems. You can follow one of the models presented on page 29, or you can design your own model. Don't forget that you can introduce new computational skills and have the students practice at home while they're working on this problem-solving unit in class.

A SIX-STEP PROCESS
▲▲▲▲▲▲▲▲▲▲▲▲▲▲▲▲

Interpret: Read the problem and summarize what you are trying to find out. What is the essence of the problem?

Gather: Collect any facts you might need to solve the problem. You may have to look in a variety of places.

Choose: Select a technique that might help you to solve the problem.

Experiment: Try the technique you've chosen. If it doesn't work, you may want to consider a different technique.

Solve: Complete the problem using the chosen technique. Present the solution clearly so others can understand your reasoning.

Interpret: Go back to the first step to review the original problem and to make sure the solution makes sense.

▲ Demonstration Problems ▲

Students are frequently asked to create and present projects. Techniques learned in math for planning, measuring, or creating these projects will be useful to them in other classes. Here are three problems that require use of these skills.

Book Covers: An artistically talented and enterprising student plans to open a business selling hand-painted report covers to other students. The posterboard to be used comes in sheets that are 32" by 36". The entrepreneur has to figure out the best way to cut out the most covers from each piece of posterboard.

Calendars: You'd like to draw a blank calendar so that you can copy it and fill in the top portions with artwork to make a gift for a friend. The calendar will have a border encompassing seven days across and five weeks down. In order to make the calendar look good, the space on the page has to be divided evenly, and straight lines need to be drawn.

Bookshelves: A student's parents have agreed to build her a set of bookshelves, provided that she make a drawing showing plans for the shelves and listing materials required. The shelves, which need to fit in a five-foot wide space, will be cut from 12" wide boards that are each 8' long. (The teacher should specify the number of books and/or other materials that must be stored on the shelves.) How many boards will be needed? Which pieces for the shelves will be cut from each board?

Sample Student Contract

Problems: Students must complete a total of eight problems, and six will be evaluated. A minimum of three problems must be completed with a partner, and a minimum of two must be completed independently. Each problem is worth 25 points and will be scored by both the teacher and the student on the evaluation forms.

Problem	Teacher	Student
Goodbye, Spy! (25)		
Doodles of Poodles (25)		
Bye, Bye, Bunnies! (25)		
Cupcake Clutter (25)		
Student's Choice:		
Student's Choice:		
Sub-total		

Spice It Up: The creation of many great products in job settings results from a combination of left-brained analytical thinking and right-brained creative thinking. Students will explore the latter by completing four *Spice It Up* activities as part of this unit. Each activity is worth up to ten points based on the amount of work, the attention to detail, and the overall quality of the finished project.

From Which Problem	Teacher	Student
Sub-total		

Final Scores: In addition to the problems, students must put their new skills to work by writing original problems, completing a home project, and solving problems on a test.

Description	Teacher	Student
Problems (150 points)		
Spice It Up (40 points)		
Original Problem (10 points)		
Home Project (50 points)		
Test (50 points)		
Total (300 points possible)		

Percentage Points _____   Final Grade _____

LINKS TO OTHER MATH TOPICS

Look for opportunities to let students put their new skill to work. Here are some ideas on how drawings can be incorporated into the presentation of traditional math topics.

▲ Multiplication & Division ▲

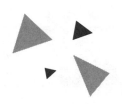

Speed-distance-time, area, and volume problems are just a few examples of problems solved with multiplication or division. These same problems can also be represented with drawings and models. Students should experiment with visual techniques to truly understand the relationships of quantities within these problems, rather than memorizing operations to use based on cue words.

Example: *A student rides her jet-powered skateboard at a rate of 30 mph. How long will it take her to go 180 miles?*

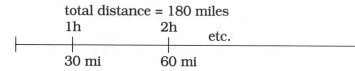

The drawing shows the total distance divided into equal segments, each representing 30 miles and one hour. This drawing leads to the conclusion that the 180 miles must be divided by 30 to get 6 hours. You can first use a drawing to help a student understand why division is used for this problem, and then you can lead the student to a generalization of the relationship.

▲ Ratios & Scale Drawing ▲

Scale drawings using equivalent ratios are created to solve problems that are inaccessible to students who are using other methods. Refer to the problems on pages 36, 41, and 48.

▲ Measurement ▲

Measurements should always be taught in context or for a purpose. Projects that need a design should include drawings through dimensions. Through such drawings, people communicate design information to one another.

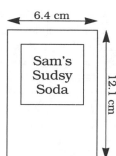

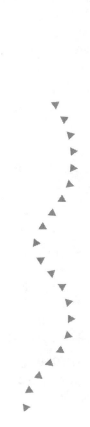

HOME PROJECT: Remodeling/Redecorating Project

Project Options

Project	Description
Tile or Carpet	Make a plan to tile or carpet the entire floor of a room in your home. You must choose a room with a shape other than a rectangle.
Wallpaper	Make a plan to wallpaper a room. Your plan will need to account for windows, doors, and other obstacles.
A New Wall	Make a plan to build a new wall to make two rooms out of one. Your plan must include a new door in either the new or an existing wall.
Your Own Idea	Create your own redecorating or remodeling project. Submit your idea with an outline of your plan to your teacher.

Here's How You Can Earn Points	Points
FAIR WARNING: This project requires that you visit a store to find the costs of materials. Parents should not be penalized if you wait until the last minute to complete this step. The project is due _____. You will be rewarded for giving your parents enough time to help you. If your parents sign this sheet and you return it tomorrow, you will earn 5 points. Every day after that, you will receive 1 point less for acquiring a signature. After 6 days, you will begin to accumulate a negative score.	5
DRAWING and MEASUREMENTS: Prepare a neat and attractive poster-size drawing of the area you plan to remodel or redecorate. Show all the needed dimensions to calculate the amount of materials required.	10
MATERIALS LIST: Prepare a list of materials required to complete your imaginary project. Describe how material is sold—by the yard, by the dozen, and so on. Include cost of adhesives, fasteners, and special tools required.	5
COST ESTIMATE: Prepare a poster giving a step-by-step explanation of how you calculated the amounts of materials required. Remember to label all quantities.	10
PRESENTATION: Pretend that the class members are potential clients who have asked you to make a presentation to convince them that you're the best person to do this job. Present your drawings, materials list, and cost estimates. Prepare sketches showing what the room will look like before and after you've completed your work. Remember to make your posters and writing large enough for everyone to read. You will earn points for the quality of your displays (5 pts) and the clarity of your explanations (5 pts).	10
STUDENT REVIEW: Following your presentation, a team of students will review your drawings and calculations and will reward you with 0-5 points for the accuracy of your work and 0-5 points for the organization and clarity of your work.	10

Redecorating/Remodeling Project Evaluation

Description	Points
FAIR WARNING The project description sheet was signed and returned on Day _____	/5
DRAWINGS AND MEASUREMENTS:	/10
MATERIALS LIST:	/5
COST ESTIMATES:	/10
PRESENTATION: Display Quality: _____ Clarity of Explanation: _____	/10
STUDENT REVIEW:	/10
TOTAL	/50

Technique A—Solution Evaluation

Name: Problem # _____ Score _____ Self Score _____	
Rate each of the following components of the solution on scale of 1 (low) - 5 (high):	
GATHER: Care was taken to collect all the information needed to solve the problem.	
CHOOSE/EXPERIMENT: Diagrams were used to solve or explain the problem.	
SOLVE: The solution was worked out carefully in organized steps.	
INTERPRET: The answer made sense in light of the facts and the original question.	
The answer is correct (3 points). The overall presentation is neat (2 points).	
Comment:	

Self-Evaluation: How Do I Rate?

How well did I gather necessary information?	
How hard did I work on this problem without giving up, even when stuck?	
How much did I use drawings while solving this problem?	
How carefully did I think about my final solution to make sure it was sensible?	
How do I feel about the quality and accuracy of my solution?	
How interesting was the problem? How hard was the probem?	

A Mouse in the House

After her trip to DisneyWorld, Anna could think of nothing but Mickey Mouse. She dreamt of Mickey, sang about Mickey, and even accidentally called her father Mickey at the dinner table. Anna was disappointed when directory assistance was unable to give her Mickey's phone number, so she decided to cheer herself up by decorating her room with a Mickey theme. Drapes, wallpaper, bedspreads—everything would become Mickey!

In a catalog, she found a set of 9-inch square, white, floor tiles with smiling Mickey faces on them, and she thought they would look great in a checkerboard pattern, alternating with black tiles. Unfortunately, her parents were unwilling to give her the $24.95 per dozen required, so Anna saved her babysitting money and was able to buy enough tiles for her 12' by 15' bedroom on her own. How many tiles did she need? If tiles are sold in packages of a dozen, how much did Anna spend?

Spice It Up!

Design and draw one of the following tiles to cover the floor of your room:
- a tile that will be the envy of all your friends
- a tile that's incedibly UGLY
- a tile nobdy would ever step on
- a tile that shows something you like

Goodbye, Spy!

The day after Everett confided in his friend Drew about the girl he had a crush on, he found posters announcing this fact being distributed on the school bus. Everett immediately suspected his sister of listening in on his phone conversation, and he decided to buy an intercom kit and some wire. From now on, conversations would be private. The problem was, how much wire should he buy? He wanted to buy enough wire, but he didn't want to spend too much money. His window and Drew's were both 15 feet off the ground, and the houses were 32 feet apart. he planned on burying the wire in a 1 foot trench. He wanted to be able to install the intercoms on any wall of the bedrooms, which were each about 12 feet square. How much wire should Everett buy?

Spice It Up!

Choose one:

1. Invent a window-to-window communication system. Demonstrate your system by sending a secret message given to you by your teacher.
2. Prepare an ad or the package for an intercom system used to prevent siblings from spying.

Bushes That Bite

"Who are you talking to, dear?" asked Ms. O'Leary from her window. Kass wasn't really talking to anyone. Yelling was more like it. She was trying to plant barberry bushes along Ms. O'Leary's driveway, but these bushes had long, sharp thorns that "bit" when she tried to handle them. So, Kass had been yelling at the bushes to "knock it off," and she had been wishing Ms. O'Leary preferred a kinder plant, like azaleas. "Oh, I'm just talking to myself," Kass told her client.

Kass had been doing yard work all summer to save for a new bike, and Ms. O'Leary had asked her to plant a row of barberry bushes on each side of her driveway. She specified to Kass that there should be a 1-foot space between the bushes, which would each grow to be about 2 feet in diameter. How many bushes did Kass have to order for this job?

Choose one:

1. Decorate your work with a mini-garden.
2. Record a radio drama or make a drawing entitled "The Attack of the Barberry Bushes."
3. Draw a picture of a bike you would like to own, complete with accessories.

Park-o-Mania

Do you have parents who are fanatics about finding the best parking space? Have you driven around the parking lot for what seems like hours just to save an extra 30 seconds of walking?

My name's Tim and I'm the son of park-o-maniacs. Park-o-mania, appearing mostly in adults, begins with an innocent desire to save a little time. For some adults, this desire turns into an unquenchable thirst for the ultimate parking space. In its later stages, park-o-mania can cause some adults to forget why they came to the store.

Both of my parents are park-o-maniacs, so going to the mall with both of them recently was a nightmare! The parking lot was completely empty, but they still couldn't agree on the best spot. The doors of the two stores we wanted to go to are 25 yards apart, and the driveway between the sidewalk and the parking lot is 10 yards wide. My parents argued about the spot that would give them the shortest overall walk. Can you find the best spot? What's the shortest walking distance from the car to Store 1, to Store 2, and back to the car?

Choose one:
1. Write a short description of a clever strategy for getting the ultimate parking spot.
2. Write a rap about finding a great parking space.
3. Draw a close-up view of a park-o-maniac in search of the ideal spot.

Executive Blocks

Katie's dad believes in remaining young at heart. She likes this quality about him, but sometimes he takes it a bit too far. "Dad," she tells him, "it's okay if you ride your bike with us, but do you have to ring the bell so often?"

Mr. Driscoll's son, Doug, feels just like Katie. He likes it when his dad stays up late playing board games with him, but when his friends are over and his dad gets the high score on the video game, it's embarrassing and discouraging.

Nevertheless, Mr. Driscoll's young spirit makes him fun to be around. The people at his office have gotten used to how he plays with blocks during lunch. He has a set of 1-inch colored cubes that he cut and painted himself, and he makes buildings and designs with them. He says the blocks relax him.

Once he had the staff trying to figure out a problem he had made up. He built a tower with yellow blocks that was 2 inches wide by 2 inches long by 16 inches tall. He claimed that he could take the tower apart and make a new one, using all the blocks, for which all three dimensions would be the same as each other. Marcie, the receptionist, finally figured it out. Can you find the dimensions of the new tower?

Choose one:
1. Draw a cartoon or describe how a parent or member of your family is young at heart.
2. Draw yourself as an adult doing something that is "kid-like."
3. Decorate your work as though you were five years old.

Doodles of Poodles

"But cartoons are my life," Ross told Mr. Winthrop, his teacher, when he was asked to stop doodling all over the sides of his tests. Since then, they've reached an understanding. Ross is allowed to doodle as long as it's not interfering with his listening and as long as the doodles aren't offensive. With time, Mr. Winthrop has come to respect Ross's drawing. He has brought him books about cartooning and even *encourages* him to use cartoons in his work.

Recently Ross wrote an essay about the underrated intelligence of poodles, and he ended up with a little extra space at the bottom of the last page. He decided a comic strip would fill the space nicely and would liven up the report.

The comic strip he planned was four frames long. Mr. Winthrop had given him tips on using a ruler to measure and draw comic strip frames so they would look neater. Knowing that he had to leave a 1-inch margin on each side of the 8 1/2-inch page, Ross made some measurements and drew four equal frames across the page. How wide was each frame? Draw them.

Spice It Up!

Choose one:
1. Write a part of Ross's poodle essay.
2. Draw a poodle comic strip in the frames you made.
3. Prepare a speech for the world's first talking poodle.

Bye, Bye, Bunnies!

When you're eleven years old, having a friend discover your room is decorated with pink dancing-bunnies wallpaper is almost as embarrassing as having her discover you still wear pajamas with feet. That's why Denise planned to redecorate her room with a new theme: music. Her parents gave her permission to glue 12-inch record albums she had collected from garage sales right over the bunny wallpaper. Her grandfather, who used to own a diner, gave Denise an old jukebox he had saved in his basement.

Before she started gluing records to the wall, Denise did a little planning. The wall was 8' high by 12 1/2' wide and had a single window. The window was 2' wide by 30" high. The top left corner was 20" from the ceiling and 4' from the left side of the wall. First, Denise had to locate the jukebox, which was 30" wide by 42" tall. Then she could locate all the records. Draw a plan showing the location of the jukebox and records on the wall. How many records are required for your plan?

Spice It Up!

Choose one:
1. Sketch a wall in your room decorated with bizarre or interesting objects.
2. List at least ten interesting uses for 100 records. Illustrate one of these uses.
3. Draw a section of wallpaper that you would be embarrassed to have your friends see on your wall.

A Treat for the Feet

"**C**arpeting? Yes!!!" Denise screamed when her parents suggested putting carpeting in her room. Denise's mother had found a store that was going out of business and was selling stock at great prices. The only catch was that Denise's family would have to install the carpeting themselves.

When they went to the store, Denise found a soft black carpeting that would go perfectly with the records on the wall, even though her mother worried that it would show dust. The roll was 12 feet wide. The manager explained that the length of carpeting would have to be the width of the roll. The store wouldn't cut an irregular shape out of the roll.

Denise's parents wanted her to be a part of the project by figuring out how many feet they should buy. Denise measured her room, as shown in the diagram. The manager explained how to join pieces together with seaming tape, but pointed out that the number of seams should be minimized. How should Denise cut pieces to carpet her room? How many feet of carpet should she and her parents buy?

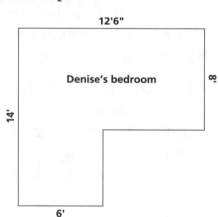

Denise's bedroom

12'6"

14'

8'

6'

Spice It Up!

Choose one:
1. Trace the room diagram and color it with your own carpet design. Go wild!
2. Write a paragraph about crossing your bedroom floor from an ant's point of view.
3. Make and model a hat from carpet scraps.

Fine Feathered Friend?

Crows think they know everything, and they always have to be right. Baldwin, the crow that lives on our block, is the most arrogant of them all. Today I have to feed him half of my sandwich because I lost a bet with him.

Baldwin asked me if I knew the expression "as the crow flies." I told him I had heard it, but I didn't know what it meant. He said that the shortest distance between two points is always as the crow flies—that is, a straight line. Our discussion ended in a bet. He said that he could give me a 3-block headstart and still get to the sandwich shop before I could. Since we had raced before, I knew that I could ride my bike just as fast as Baldwin could fly. I took the bet.

All our streets run north-south or east-west, and the shop is 6 blocks east and 8 blocks north. I lost both races. The first time, I rode directly east for 6 blocks and then directly north for 8 blocks. The next time I tried zig-zagging. Both times he was laughing when I got there. Can you tell how many blocks Baldwin beat me by?

Spice It Up!

Choose one:

1. Illustrate part of this story.
2. Make up a story based on another common expression, and be ready to share it.
3. Briefly describe a conversation you might have with a bird.
4. Draw your best friend as a bird.

Cupcake Clutter

"**C**lean up your room today!" Eva's mother yelled up the stairs. "And I want all those cupcakes picked up and put in boxes!" She was, of course, referring to Eva's collection of 420 cupcakes. Why couldn't her daughter collect stamps or stickers like other kids? Eva was about to holler an objection to her mom's request down the stairs, but as she climbed out of bed and put her feet into her slippers, she felt cool cupcake frosting ooze between her toes. Now how did that get in there? she wondered. Perhaps putting away the cupcakes wasn't such a bad idea after all. In the basement, Eva was able to find some empty boxes that measured 18" by 31". The cupcake dimensions are shown below. Can you figure out how many boxes it took Eva to put away all her cupcakes?

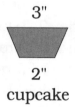

3"

2"

cupcake

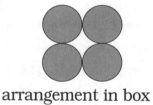

arrangement in box

CHALLENGE: If Eva turned every other cupcake upside-down, the cupcakes would fit more snugly. How many boxes would it take to pack the cupcakes this way?

Spice It Up!

Choose one:
1. Bake some cupcakes for the class. Be creative in decorating them.
2. Create an original cupcake recipe, and draw a picture of the finished product.
3. Write an excuse that explains why you didn't bake for the class.

T.J. in Fabricland

T.J. learned how to make quilts from his grandmother when he stayed at her house one summer. She helped him make a mini-quilt for his stuffed bear. Now he is planning to make his first full-sized quilt for his sister for the holidays.

T.J.'s family has a tradition of drawing names from a hat and making a present for the person whose name is drawn. They find that hand-made presents add an extra touch of warmth to the giving of gifts. Last year T.J. made a birdhouse from a kit for his dad, and the year before he sewed a small bunny for his youngest sister. At 72" by 78", the quilt for his sister will be T.J.'s biggest present yet.

The finished quilt will be made from 6" squares of different types of fabric, alternating in a checkerboard pattern. To allow for seams, each square will have an extra 1/4" border of fabric. T.J. knows that fabric comes off the bolt (or roll) in 45" widths. He wants to be sure to buy a long piece of each type of fabric plus some extra fabric to allow for mistakes. What length of each 45" wide fabric should he buy?

CHALLENGE: If fabric is sold in lengths of 1/4 yard and costs $3.40 per yard, about how much will the fabric for the quilt cost?

> 6" square
> with 1/4"
> border

Spice It Up!

Design one of these quilts:
- a quilt that would keep you warm if it snowed in your bedroom
- a quilt that would keep you cool
- a quilt that would scare you in your sleep
- a quilt with electronic extras

Emma's Dilemma

The bucketful of colored cubes spilled to the floor at our feet. The four of us leaned forward just enough to see them lying on our shoes. "Why'd you do that?" my cousin Hillary asked my Aunt Emma. "You look bored," she said, "so I've got a math puzzle for you." We all groaned and fell back into the sofa cushions. We were bored, but not bored enough for another one of her math puzzles. "And the winner gets to come out for banana splits with me," Aunt Emma added. We sat back up again, and she explained the puzzle:

We were each given 64 blocks with which to build a rectangular tower that would appear square when viewed from above. The winner would be the person who built the tower requiring the least amount of paint to cover its five exposed sides. In other words, our towers should have as few squares facing out as possible. Since we each had the same number of blocks, I thought that every tower would have the same number of sides on the outside, but I was wrong. Build four different designs, and calculate the number of sides facing out for each. Determine which design would win Aunt Emma's contest.

Spice It Up!

Choose one of the following:
1. Draw or describe a mega-sundae that you'd like as a reward.
2. Sketch your partner trapped in a clear cube.
3. Use a single piece of paper to build the most beautiful cube in the world.

Better Than Babysitting

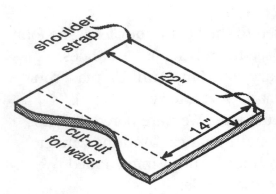

shoulder strap

22"

14"

cut-out for waist

Keith and his friend Amber were discouraged by the time it took them to earn money by babysitting and cutting lawns. They brainstormed until they came up with the idea of selling drinks at the town ballfield. Baseball was the lifeblood of their town; it gave people a game to watch and a place to talk with friends. Even Little League drew crowds of several hundred people.

Amber lived across the street from the field, so they kept the drinks cold in her basement refrigerator. Keith designed a tray to hold the filled cups, so he and Amber could walk through the stands to sell them. His initial design is shown. The holes are 2.5 inches across to hold the cups. Design a tray that will hold as many cups as possible, but will still have enough wood between the cups so the tray won't break easily. Draw the tray from above with dimensions to show where the holes should be cut.

3"

2.5"

drink cup

Spice It Up!

Suppose that you are entering a nationwide contest. You must submit a plan for a business you can run during the summer. The winner receives $10,000 to begin the business. Write your business proposal, including a description of how you will spend the money.

Matt's Metaphor Rebuttal

Ms. Oles turned away from the board where she was illustrating the life cycle of sea worms to see 25 students slumped in their chairs or draped across their desks in assorted postures of boredom. "Trying to get you to do any work on a hot Friday afternoon is like fitting a square peg into a round hole," she said. Jason raised his hand.

"Please don't think I'm trying to be rude, Ms. Oles, but I'm not sure that's right." he said. The rest of the class sat up in anticipation of whatever entertainment Jason had in store for them today. "I think a square peg can fit into a round hole just fine."

"Oh, you do?" Ms. Oles asked, trying to hide the fact that she was welcoming a break as much as her students were. "Well, would you care to explain?"

"It's simple," Jason said with a smile. "All you need is a small enough peg or a large enough hole." Ms. Oles smiled back. Find the diameter of the smallest hole a 10 cm square peg could fit through.

Spice It Up!

Choose one:
1. Think of another well-known expression such as "Two wrongs don't make a right" and explain why it's not exactly correct.
2. Decorate your work with square pegs and round holes.

Pie Surprise

D*esign a game based on life in your family.* Bianca could hardly believe that her teacher had given this assignment. She knew immediately that her game, Pie Surprise, would be chance to get back at her brother for all the tricks he had played on her over the years.

She made a gameboard similar to Monopoly™. The playing pieces represented sisters, and there was one space on each side of the board that showed a brother's face. The goal was to buy pies at the bakeries on the corners and "deposit" them on the brother spaces. The first player to deposit one of each pie type on each brother was the winner.

Bianca wanted to make the gameboard look as neat as possible, so she did a lot of planning on her 2' by 2' sheet of cardboard. She wanted the corners to be 3-inch squares, and she wanted 8 equal side-spaces between every two corners. She figured that a card set on a side-space should have a 1/4" border around it. Show the dimensions of a side-space and of a card that would fit into this side-space.

Angela's gameboard

Choose one:
1. Describe what your game would be about if you were given Angela's assignment.
2. Draw one side space from Angela's game.
3. Write your theory on why brothers and sisters play tricks on each other.

Sister Shelter

For years Marco had been teasing his sister, but now she was learning to defend herself. First there was the game she made for class in which sisters threw pies at brothers. Now she was threatening a real pie attack. With holiday pie season coming up, what could Marco do? Stopping the teasing was one solution, but Marco had another idea: a sister shelter!

Marco used his own money, saved from shoveling snow from driveways, to buy concrete blocks for the shelter. The blocks were 16" long by 8" high by 7 1/2" wide. The finished shelter was 12' long, 10' 7" wide, and 6' 8" high. It had a plywood roof, and the only entrance was through a tunnel. How many blocks were required for the first layer of the shelter? How many blocks were required for the entire shelter?

CHALLENGE: Redesign the shelter with a 32" by 64" door and a 2' square window.

Spice It Up!

Choose one:
1. Sketch the ultimate shelter for protecting yourself from your sibling.
2. Write a set of instructions that your brother or sister could follow to become your ideal sibling.
3. Write a rap about the tricks siblings play on each other.

Dream Dwelling

Nate's recent dream about his own apartment is definitely going into his Dream Hall-of-Fame. It was so cool! In the dream, his parents told him that it was time that he lived on his own. "Unfortunately," they said, "you have to go to school, so we'll give you all the money you need to rent an apartment, decorate it, and buy stereo equipment and food. Okay?" Nate agreed. His grandparents gave him a car in the dream, and the governor granted Nate a special license so he could drive it.

MEASUREMENTS	
• bed	.5' x 7'
• desk	.2' x 4'
• bureau	.2' x 3'
• video game	.2' 6" x 3'
• hot tub	.8' x 7'
• computer table	.2' 6" x 3' 6"
• bookshelf	.1' x 6'

The bedroom in Nate's dream apartment was awesome. The dimensions of the furniture are shown. Nate wondered if all that stuff really would have fit in the bedroom. After all, he remembered being told that the bedroom was 14' by 20', with a 2' 6" door located near one of the corners.

Using furniture and a room drawn to scale, figure out whether or how Nate could arrange things. Make sure you leave space to walk around, open the door, and really use the furniture. When you complete your design, tape or glue the scale furniture down or redraw the room arrangement.

Spice It Up!

Choose one:
1. Sketch a plan for your ideal apartment.
2. Illustrate a scene from an imaginary dream from your Dream Hall of Fame.
3. Draw or describe what you would choose to dream about.

In the Doghouse

Doug looked through the water-streaked window into the gray, drizzly afternoon. His dog, also named Doug, sat in a puddle on the end of his chain, looking with large eyes at the warm glow coming from his master's window. He whimpered and waved his paw in the air, splashing water into his nose when his paw hit the ground again. Doug watched his drenched pooch and made up his mind—as soon as there was a sunny day, he would build his best friend a doghouse.

He left the window and grabbed a piece of paper from his mom's desk. On the back, he sketched a plan for the doghouse. It would be 3' wide and 2'6" deep. The flat roof would slope from the front to the back and would overlap the house by about 6" on all four sides. The front wall would be 3' high, and the back would be 2' high. There would be a 1'8" square door cut out of the front, and the bottom would be open to the ground. Doug knew that plywood came in 4' by 8' sheets. It was expensive, so he wanted to use as little as possible. He drew a plan to show how he would cut out all the pieces.

Draw a plan to show how you would cut out the pieces for Doug's doghouse. How many sheets of plywood would you need to buy? What would you build with the leftover pieces?

Choose one:
1. Design an amazing house for your pet.
2. Draw a treehouse for a very unusual pet that you would like to have.
3. Write a thank-you note from Doug the dog to Doug.

Lazy Lawnmowing

Larry's idea of a perfect afternoon is a soft couch and an excellent remote channel changer. Yes, it's obvious—Larry is lazy. His parents are trying to get him to change by stopping his allowance and giving him opportunities to earn money around the house. They offered him $6.00 to cut the lawn.

Larry definitely wanted the money, but Larry didn't want to do any work. Luckily, Larry's family owned a self-propelled lawnmower. All it needed was a little direction.

Larry figured he could put a cylindrical post in the middle of the yard and then tie a cord from the post to the lawnmower. As the lawnmower traveled in a circle, the cord would wrap around the post, in effect moving the lawnmower closer to the post each time around. The lawnmower would automatically cut a spiral path in the grass.

Larry found that his lawnmower could cut an 18" wide path. He figured that each path around the yard should overlap the previous path by 2". He would be sure that no grass blades were missed. What should the diameter of the post be?

Spice It Up!

Choose one:
1. Write a letter to the governor describing why you shouldn't have to do a specific chore.
2. Create an invention that would eliminate one of your chores.
3. Draw Larry as a couch potato.

World Problems

Advice: *When filling out order forms, be very careful to write down the correct catalog numbers.* Consider the case of Principal Hardy of Slog-doggie Elementary School. Thinking she was ordering 15,000 pencils for the school, she wrote #12913 on the order form. Unfortunately, pencils are #12973, so Principal Hardy received an order of 15,000 globes, each 30 cm across. The company said they'd pick them up, but it would take a month. Meanwhile, what does a person do with that many globes?

Dana, the custodian, loved to make up problems. He talked with Ms. Nichols and her math class about storing the globes and asked how many globes they could store in their room if they took everything else out. The room was 12 m long, 9 m wide, and 3 m high. Dana told the class that the globes should be stacked as shown in the diagram, with no overlap.

Dana then pointed out that there would be room between the globes for smaller balls. He asked the students to figure out the diameter of the largest ball that could fit between every four globes. He also asked how many of these balls it would take to fill the room if all the globes were removed. Try to figure out Dana's world problems.

Spice It Up!

We've just received word that the company absolutely refuses to take back the globes. We're stuck with them! It's up to you to come up with something interesting, fun, useful, or unique that we can do with 15,000 globes. Write down at least five good ideas. Illustrate your favorite idea.

Represent it with a
DIAGRAM

4

WHAT'S THE BIG IDEA?

Diagrams are powerful tools for understanding a variety of phenomena and for planning complicated systems. Unlike drawings, which show how parts are physically related, diagrams help us to see how ideas or other non-physical elements interact with each other. With this information, we can understand and design processes, make schedules, and develop financial plans.

Here are some of the systems that diagrams help us visualize:
- motion of machines
- biological processes
- budgets and flow of money
- stresses in machines and structures
- ecosystems
- corporate organization
- air, water, and sewage systems
- decision making
- moving bodies of water
- chemical processes
- weather patterns
- schedules
- aerodynamics of vehicles
- life cycles
- shipping routes
- process control in factories
- natural resource management
- optimal use of supplies
- electrical and electronic circuits
- paths of celestial objects
- computer programs
- home plumbing and electricity
- optics and acoustics
- economics and fiscal planning

Students who have facility with diagrams can use this diagnostic tool to better understand many traditional math topics. They can learn multiplication and division through the use of diagrams before they memorize the corresponding algorithms. An understanding of percent, ratio, and probability often eludes middle school students, but diagrams allow these topics to be explored and understood on a conceptual level before students master the complex manipulation of the figures associated with each. (Refer to *Links to Other Math Topics* later in this chapter for examples of how diagrams can illuminate difficult math concepts.) Diagrams are a low-cost alternative to manipulatives, such as blocks, tiles, and counters. By strengthening skills in using diagrams, we empower students with a tool they can carry wherever they go.

WHO NEEDS HELP?
▲▲▲▲▲▲▲▲▲▲▲▲▲▲▲▲

Here are two suggestions for keeping track of students who need your help as you circulate through the room:

HELP
K.M.
Jake
Ashley
Mark

The Help Screen:
Designate an area on the board where students can write their names when they need your assistance. You can divide this help "screen" into categories that describe the type of help needed.

Signal Beacons: At the beginning of the class period, give each group a set of three cups: one yellow, one red, and one blue. The cups should nest inside one another so that students can put the cup that signals their need on the outside of the stack.
Blue = We're fine.
Yellow = Please help us when you can.
Red = Emergency, we can't do anything else until you talk with us.

PRESENTING THIS TECHNIQUE

The steps for introducing diagramming are almost the same as described for introducing drawing in Chapter 3. Re-read these steps on pages 28-29 to learn how to choose and present a set of problems. The comments below offer suggestions unique to presenting the diagramming technique for solving problems.

• Ask students to share experiences they've had in other math classes when diagrams have helped them to learn a new concept. Challenge them to show you how first graders could use diagrams to solve multiplication problems, even though they don't know how to multiply.

• Have students bring in science books or news magazines that have diagrams. They should be prepared to share and explain the diagrams they have found in these resources.

▲ **Demonstration Problems** ▲

The first demonstration problem is an example of how diagrams can be used to introduce percent problems. Students can solve this problem armed only with the knowledge that percent means "out of 100." The solution then follows the steps of the problems on page 61 and 67, later in this chapter. (The solutions to these problems can be found on pages 108–130.)

An Idea Before It's Time: Wishing to capitalize on the large numbers of allergy sufferers who would like to be dog owners, Ms. Cecily B. Hathaway invented the radio-controlled, non-allergenic dog—the perfect pet. Unfortunately, the electronic canines didn't sell like hot-cakes, and they've been marked down twice from the original $750 selling price. In the first sale, this obviously-high price was cut 20%. Ms. Hathaway then slashed this price an additional 40%. What is the current price of the dogs?

Shopping for Dad: Two daughters go separately to the same store to shop for a present for their dad's birthday. They both know what types of things their father enjoys, so each daughter will probably pick from the same ten items in the store that would most likely please their father. What are the chances that the two daughters will pick the same gift?

The Renegade Candidate: A class decided to conduct a mock presidential election within their grade level. Before the election, some students conspired to write in one of the students' names on the ballot. The student won; she received two votes for every vote received by the Democratic candidate, who in turn received two votes for every vote received by the Republican candidate. If 91 students voted, how many votes did each candidate receive?

LINKS TO OTHER MATH TOPICS

Diagrams may be the single most powerful tool for understanding math topics that you can share with your students. Here are some examples of how diagrams can be used to illustrate topics typically taught in middle grades.

▲ Multiplication ▲

Suppose the principal was in an extremely good mood and decided to give each of the 23 students in our class 4 new cars. How many new cars would we have altogether?

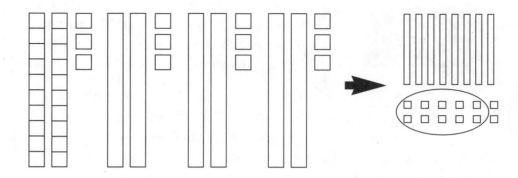

The long bars (tens) and the squares (ones) are arranged to show 23 four times. After the tens and ones are put together, some of the ones have to be grouped into a new 10. Solving multiplication problems graphically shows the meaning of regrouping, in a way that requires no previous knowledge of multiplication.

▲ Ratios ▲

"I'm really excited that my order just came in! With the money I got for my birthday, I ordered some floons and goobles, and I can't wait to use them. They come in packs containing 2 floons and 3 goobles. If I ordered 12 floons, how many goobles are there in the box?

This diagram illustrates that when you multiply one element of a ratio by a value, you have to multiply the other element by that value, too. Multiplying the 2 to 3 ratio of floons to goobles by 2, 3, 4, 5, and 6 generates the series of ratios below.

$$\frac{2}{3} = \frac{4}{6} = \frac{6}{9} = \frac{8}{12} = \frac{10}{15} = \frac{12}{18} \text{ etc.}$$

▲ Fractions ▲

Diagrams are commonly used to represent and compare fractions, but they can also be used to show operations with fractions. The following diagram shows what happens when two fractions are multiplied. Multiplying 8 by 5 could be represented by drawing 8 rows of 5 unit

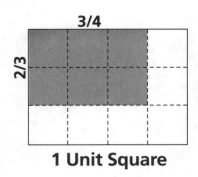

3/4

2/3

1 Unit Square

squares each, giving a total of 40 unit squares. Similarly, the diagram to the left shows (within a unit square) 2/3 of a row of 3/4 or 3/4 of a row of 2/3. The result is 3/4 x 2/3 = 6/12.

This diagram also shows why multiplying fractions requires multiplying the numerators and multiplying the denominators. The denominators of the fractions show the number of rows and the number of columns. Multiplying these values gives the total number of rectangles formed within the unit square. In this case, the unit square is divided into twelfths. The numerators give the number of shaded rows and shaded columns. In this case, 3 columns times 2 rows equals 6 shaded rectangles, or 6 twelfths.

▲ Factors, Multiples, & Primes ▲

The diagram below shows how graph paper can be used to discover multiples and factors. For the drawings on the left, students were asked to find different rectangles that would have exactly 12 squares. There were 3 combinations. If they had been asked to look for rectangles with 13 squares, they would have found only one (13 x 1), as would be the case for any prime number. The drawing on the right shows how multiples of a number are generated by the repeated addition of the same number of squares to the rectangle.

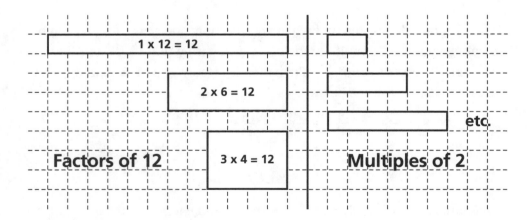

1 x 12 = 12

2 x 6 = 12

3 x 4 = 12

Factors of 12

Multiples of 2

etc.

HOME PROJECT: A Sampling of Diagrams

Directions: You must complete assignment A and either assignment B or C.

Assignment A: **You're the Teacher**

Imagine that your math students don't understand a concept you're trying to teach. You know that diagrams may help. Choose one of the math topics below, and create a diagram that will help explain it to a group of students. (You may have to research to learn about the topic you have chosen.) The teacher will ask you to prepare a presentation for the class or small group. Include your diagram in this presentation.

- multiplying two 2-digit numbers
- multiplying fractions
- converting fractions to decimals
- adding or subtracting fractions with unlike denominators
- finding the mean and median of a set of numbers
- showing the relationship between speed, distance, and time
- determining the chances of something occurring
- proving Pythagoras's theorem about the sides of a triangle
- (If you have an original idea, consult the teacher.)

- dividing by a 2-digit divisor
- dividing fractions
- converting fractions to percents

Scoring: You can receive up to 10 points for the quality, clarity, and originality of your diagram and up to 15 points for the accuracy and organization of your presentation.

Assignment B: **How Does It Work?**

Use a diagram to explain how something works in science, business, or government. Biological processes, computer programs, motions of machines, and paths of orbiting spacecraft are only a few varied examples of systems that can be explained with diagrams. Your teacher will help you brainstorm to list other ideas.

Select and research a topic. Create a diagram that will help explain your topic to others. Your teacher will ask you to prepare a short presentation for either the class or a small group. You can earn up to 25 points for your knowledge of your topic, the quality of your diagram, and the clarity of your presentation.

Assignment C: **In the News**

Find and read an article that interests you in a newspaper or news magazine. Study the diagrams and learn what they mean. The teacher will ask you to share what you learned in a presentation to either the whole class or a small group.

After you've gained a thorough understanding of your article, make an outline of the points you want to include in your summary. Make a poster-sized copy of the diagram from the article. You may add your own special touches, but give credit to the source of the diagram somewhere on your poster. You can earn up to 25 points for your knowledge of your topic, the quality of your diagram, and the clarity of your presentation.

Diagram-Project Evaluation

Description	Points
ASSIGNMENT A: DIAGRAM Your diagrams should be clear, attractive, interesting, and easy to read from the back of the room. ____/5–visual quality and clarity ____/5–creativity & originality	/10
ASSIGNMENT A: PRESENTATION Your presentation should be accurate, organized, easy to follow, and should make good use of the diagram. ____/5–accuracy ____/5–organization ____/5–diagram explanation	/15
ASSIGNMENT B or C: DIAGRAM In addition to being neatly drawn and attractive, your drawing should explain your topic well. ____/5–visual quality and clarity ____/5–explanation of topic presented	/10
ASSIGNMENT B or C: PRESENTATION Your presentation should be interesting, organized, and should show that you learned your topic well. ____/5–knowledge of topic ____/5–organization ____/5–appeal to audience	/15
TOTAL	/50

Technique B—Solution Evaluation

Name: Problem # ____ Score ____ Self Score ____	
Rate each of the following components of the solution on scale of 1 (low) - 5 (high):	
GATHER: Care was taken to collect all the information needed to solve the problem.	
CHOOSE/EXPERIMENT: Diagrams were used to solve or explain the problem.	
SOLVE: The solution was worked out carefully in organized steps.	
INTERPRET: The answer made sense in light of the facts and the original question.	
The answer is correct (3 points). The overall presentation is neat (2 points).	
Comment:	

Self-Evaluation: How Do I Rate?

How well did I gather information needed to solve the problem?	
How hard did I work on this problem without giving up, even when stuck?	
How much did I use or practice the use of diagrams while solving this problem?	
How carefully did I think about my final solution to be sure it made sense?	
How good did I feel about the quality and accuracy of my solution?	
How interesting was the problem? How hard was the probem?	

Sherlock Bothmerini

My math teacher, Ms. Bothmerini, is pretty cool in lots of ways, and she loves a good mystery. Recently she has been watching a mystery series on public television and telling us the stories.

I knew something big was going on when Ms. Bothmerini came into our class last week wearing a long overcoat—she even asked us to call her Holmes! Earlier that day, somebody had slipped worms into the school spaghetti, and "Holmes" thought it was an excellent opportunity for us to solve a *real* mystery.

The worms were put into the spaghetti by somebody in the hot lunch line during the first lunch period. We found out that only 40% of the 1000 students in the school ate during that lunch period, and only 75% of those students bought hot lunch. That helped us narrow the list of suspects. Next we learned that 3% of the hot lunch students had observed worms in Mr. Curtis's science class earlier that day. We turned our final list over to the principal, who apparently had her own way of narrowing down the suspects. Michael Nostrildorf was suspended the next day. How many students were on our list?

Spice It Up!

Choose one:

1. Prepare a monologue in which you appear as Holmes to describe how you solved the worm case or another case that you make up.
2. Write a recipe based on fresh, juicy worms. Illustrate the final dish.
3. Draw either the longest, smartest, or most attractive worm in the world.

Infected Technology

How can a computer catch cold? Meg wondered when she read the news about a computer virus that was going around. She began doing some research. Here's what she found out:

A computer programs is a set of instructions that tells the computer what to do. A virus is a program that tells the computer to do something the user doesn't want it to do, like erase files. People hide viruses in other computer files, and viruses copy themselves from computer to computer when people share "infected" files over the internet or on disks. The term *virus* describes these programs because they make computers "sick," and the problem can spread.

Meg thought it would be fun to create a virus that would make a polar bear roller skate around the screen for an hour on the first day of every month. Meg's father was upset about her plan because even though she was just trying to be funny, many people would be inconvenienced. "Suppose," he said, "that each day every infected computer spreads the virus to one other computer. If after day #1 two computers are infected, how many computers would be infected at the end of the 10th day? the 20th day?" You figure it out.

Spice It Up!

Choose one:
1. Draw what a computer virus might look like if it were a living thing.
2. Draw Meg's skating polar bear in action.
3. Dress as a computer virus and give a speech to the class about your remorse for causing damage in someone's computer.

The Clucky Winner

Laura and Alex actually like each other, but you'd never know it by watching them together. They argue about everything.

Recently, Laura and Alex were talking about their brothers and sisters. They noticed that their families are reversed—Laura has three brothers and Alex has three sisters. Alex stated that the odds were that most families with four children would have two boys and two girls. Laura disagreed, of course. She claimed that there was a better chance of three children of one sex and one of the other.

Over lunch, the debate grew hotter and hotter, finally resulting in a bet. Laura and Alex declared that the loser of the bet would have to stand up on a chair and cluck like a chicken during lunch. They went to see their favorite teacher, Ms. Spaulding, hoping that she would know the answer. She suggested that they draw a diagram to figure it out.

Laura and Alex both solved the problem later that day. One of them was the lucky winner, and the other was the "clucky" winner. Who was right?

Spice It Up!

Choose one:
1. Write a letter from Laura to Alex boasting about how *you* are right once again.
2. Suppose you started a business appearing at birthday parties as the Dancing Chicken. Make a yellow pages ad describing your service.
3. At home, prepare a video of yourself doing your very best chicken imitation.

Dazed By Dollars

Mark is afraid of numbers, so when he had a night-mare in which a giant seven put him in a taco shell and ate him, he hired his younger sister as his accountant. He pays her $1.50 per week to face his weekly financial confusion described below.

Mark and his brother each get a $3.75 allowance, but in exchange for secretly eating his brother's vegetables during dinner, he gets one-third of his brother's allowance. Mark's grandmother pays both him and his college account $7.50 for cutting her lawn. From this income, Mark has to pay his dad $1.75 for lawnmower expenses. He also has to pay his dad $2.25 per week for two expensive ties he ruined in a magic trick that fizzled.

Mark puts half of his net weekly income into his college account. For each dollar Mark saves, his parents put in $1.50. Also, Mark's dad has been secretly depositing the lawnmower money into this account. Draw a diagram to show the flow of money between Mark, his family members, and his savings account. What is the weekly increase in Mark's college account? What would this amount be if Mark didn't hire an accountant?

Spice It Up!

Choose one:
1. Illustrate Mark's bad taco dream.
2. Make a comic strip portraying Mark's mishap with his dad's ties.
3. Write a scene in which one or two characters encounter a "dangerous" number.

Candid Confectioner

While eating a Munchie Oats Health Bar, Sara read on the label that sugar was the most abundant ingredient in what the title implied was a healthy snack. "If they're going to make it with lots of sugar, why can't they just be honest about it?" she asked herself. That's when she decided to start her own honestly unhealthy snack business—the X. S. Sugar Company—in her basement.

In addition to having fun, Sara is learning about running a business. For example, right now she is faced with unexpected expenses for delivering the goodies to customers in four towns (shown below). Her trucks get 12 miles to the gallon, and gas costs $1.35 per gallon. They live in Dentureville and make daily deliveries to the other towns. They would like to minimize the total travel distance to save money on gas. Find the best and worst routes they could take. By taking the best route, how many miles do they save per day? In one year (250 work days), how much money can they save?

Dentureville
•

Caninus
•
Acavity •

•
Bicuspid

	D	C	B
A	42	105	45
B	90	147	
C	120		

Spice It Up!

Choose one:
1. Write a recipe for one of the company's treats.
2. Draw a close-up of the teeth of a person who has been eating Candid Confectioner goodies for 5 years.
3. Create a logo for the company.

Meeting Ms. Right

Jordan found a way to mix his favorite two subjects—math and girls. For his math project, he decided to use a scientific approach to choose the person he would ask to the upcoming dance. Jordan decided that his date should have hazel eyes and be shorter than he is. Jordan's father was the school nurse, so Jordan was able to sneak into the school health records. He found that only 15% of the 800 students in the school had hazel eyes, and only 30% of the hazel-eyed students were shorter than he is. Only 50% of the people still on the list were girls.

Jordan eliminated one-third of the remaining students because they were in the grade above his, and he was too nervous to ask them out. His "spies" gave him a list of the girls who didn't want to go to the dance with him. He figured it would be pointless to ask these girls out, so he was able to cross off three-quarters of the people on his current list.

Jordan finally asked out each girl on the completed list. His first invitations were rejected, but the last girl he asked, said yes. Jordan did get an A on his math project.

How many girls turned down Jordan's invitation?

Spice It Up!

Choose one:
1. Design a unique invention that asks someone to dance for you.
2. Write a love letter to an imaginary person that expresses your affection in terms of percentages.

Maya's Early Retirement

Maya can talk to her parents about anything. She's planning on retiring before she's thirty years old, and her parents are going to help her.

What's Maya going to do? Open her own business, of course. She designed a fluffy stuffed yellow thing called a Gluzzie that looks like a cross between a squirrel and a banana. She started by making a few for her friends, who went absolutely wild over them. It has turned into a fad, and Maya sees this as her big chance to start a career. She'll be opening her first factory in the fall.

Maya is planning a 3-step assembly line for making the Gluzzies. The first step is to cut out the fabric, which a person can do at the rate of 10 patterns per hour. Next, the fabric is sewed and stuffed. This is the slowest step; each person can sew and stuff only 6 Gluzzies per hour. The last step, putting on eyes and yellow fuzz, is easy. Each person can add these finishing touches to 15 Gluzzies per hour. Maya's Dad has helped her find 30 old school desks that she will make into work stations, with a worker doing one of the steps at each station. She has to decide how many of the 30 employees should be assigned to each step so that her factory can produce as many Gluzzies per hour as possible. How many people would *you* assign to each step? With your plan, how many Gluzzies would be produced during each 8-hour work day?

Spice It Up!

Choose one:
1. Make a Gluzzie, the packaging for a Gluzzie, or a Gluzzie advertisement.
2. Create and display an original product that you could make in your own factory.
3. Write a catchy advertising jingle for Gluzzies. Be prepared to sing in class.

Inspecting Mibzopplers

Dad is an inventor, but his inventions also embarrass me. For a year now, he's been setting up a factory to manufacture his latest invention, the mibzoppler. I don't even know what it does! Dad says that it's a secret but that it will pay for my college education and much more. So now he's asking *me* to help get the factory ready.

My first job is to assign each of the 15 people he hired to inspect mibzopplers, coming out of 1 of 5 machines at the rate of 150 per hour. The employees work at different speeds. He tested the employees and found they could inspect 65, 60, 60, 55, 55, 55, 50, 50, 45, 45, 45, 45, 40, 40, and 30 mibzopplers per hour. I'm supposed to divide the employees among the 5 machines in a way that will allow us to inspect as many mibzopplers per hour as possible. I'm also supposed to tell Dad how many mibzopplers will be left to inspect at the end of a 7-hour shift. Help me!

A Mibzoppler

Spice It Up!

Choose one:
1. List at least ten possible uses for the mibzoppler.
2. The mibzoppler shown is the basic model. Draw a deluxe mibzoppler.
3. Build a real mibzoppler and demonstrate it to the class as though you are a traveling salesperson.

Games for Grades

Last week I got a B on my probability test, and Ms. McGill has offered to play a game with me that might lower or raise this grade. I don't know whether I should take this offer or not.

Here's how it works: Ms. McGill will play a card game with anyone who wants to try to raise the test grade. If the student wins, the grade goes up 1 letter; if Ms. McGill wins, the grade goes down 1 letter. The student and Ms. McGill each start with 50 marbles. In the center of the table is a pack of 8 cards and a can in which the winner of each round of the game puts a marble. In the pack of cards are 2 each of the ace, jack, queen, and king. The pack is shuffled and two cards are drawn at random. If the cards are not identical, Ms. McGill puts a marble into the can, but if the cards *are* identical, the student puts 5 marbles into the can. The 8 cards are reshuffled after each round, and whoever puts all of his or her marbles into the can first is the winner.

It seems like a good idea to me, because the students get to put in more marbles when *they* win rounds; maybe Ms. McGill is trying to help us. But, then again, probability has to do with chances that things will happen, so maybe the point is for us to use what we've learned about probability to figure out who has a better chance of winning. Can you figure out if I should play or not?

Choose one:
1. Draw a marble with an illustration of this problem on it.
2. Design a similar game in which it appears that your opponent has the advantage but you're the one who really has the slight edge.

The Pedaling Editor

Julie knows that "a lot" is two words, not one. She was the only one in her third grade class who could spell it correctly. Well, maybe it wasn't that big a deal when she was little, but now her writing skills help her earn big bucks. Other students pay her to edit the drafts of their reports

Although she refuses to *write* other people's papers, she will, for the appropriate fee, show people how to change specific sentences and paragraphs to make their writing sound more clear, concise, and interesting. She's also great at finding all the punctuation, grammar, and spelling errors.

Unfortunately, Julie has competition; another student named Jaylyn is also offering editing services. To try to win the race for customers, Julie offers to ride her bike to clients' houses at any time of the day or night to help them edit papers. In order to get to their houses quickly, Julie has planned out the shortest routes to various points in town. For instance, if Julie lives at A (in the diagram), what is the shortest route she can take to reach the house at B?

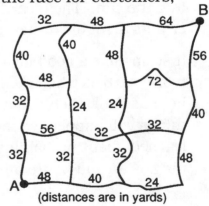

(distances are in yards)

Spice It Up!

Choose one:

1. Write a paragraph to challenge Julie. It must be readable, but it must have at least 5 errors. Try also to make it amusing.
2. Make the map larger, and add details from the neighborhood to make it more exciting. Locate Julie on her bike on your map.

Trent's Tongue Tricks

I never should have asked Trent what the strange-looking lunchmeat in his sandwich was. I was so repulsed when he told me it was beef tongue that I had to go sit at another table. One of my policies is to never taste food that can taste you back. For as long as I can remember, Trent has had a fascination with tongues. In second grade when everybody else was dressed like pirates, princesses, or monsters for Halloween, Trent dressed like a tongue. Tasteful, huh?

Last month, Trent did his science project on tongues. As part of his project, he surveyed 200 students to see what tongue tricks they could do. He found that 45% of the group could curl their tongues but only 15% could say, "I wish I could wash my Irish wrist watch" ten times without stopping or making a mistake. The overlap of these two groups represented 5% of the people surveyed. Determine the number of people out of the 200 who couldn't do either trick. What percent of the group did these students represent?

Spice It Up!

Choose one:
1. After trying the tongue twisters in the problem and its title, make a poster with a few tongue twisters that you write yourself.
2. Illustrate Trent trying to eat his sandwich as it tries to eat him back.
3. Draw a picture of Trent on Halloween.

A Lion and His Socks

As the wedding march played and Margaret walked down the aisle on the arm of her father, Joe, the eyes of the invited guests were on Joe's socks. The left sock was green and the right was red. "I have another pair just like it at home," he joked at the reception.

This was a tradition—red and green socks on weekends and on special occasions. It started when Joe's daughters were little and gave him socks in ultra-bright colors. "What should I do with these?" he asked his wife. She told him Rule Number Five of parenting: You must wear or use any gift that your small child draws, makes, or finds for you, even if friends or strangers point at you and giggle.

From that day, Joe has worn brightly colored socks on weekends, a different color on each foot. Somewhere along the way, he specialized in only red and green socks. As the Lt. Governor of the Lions Club, he even tried to have these brightly colored socks, along with lion slippers, adopted as part of the official Lions Club uniform.

Being a puzzle lover, Joe made up challenges having to do with all of his colored socks. For example, if he has 4 red socks and 4 green socks in a drawer and if every day he pulls out 2 socks with his eyes closed, about how many times in a year will he pull out socks that don't match?

Draw (or make) one of the following pairs of socks:

- socks with incredible colors.
- socks that are UGLIER than all other socks.
- socks that are more beautiful than any other.
- socks to attract animals or birds.

See What I Saw

I don't have any out-of-focus pictures to prove it, but Bigfoot is real. And believe it or not, he's actually a fun guy. Yesterday at dusk when I went back to the playground to get a ball I had left there, I found Bigfoot swinging and—here's the unbelievable part—giggling. It's not what I expected from a 868-lb hairy beast. We became fast friends, and we played together for over an hour. One word of caution: never ask a Bigfoot to give you a push on a swing! Going all the way around is bit scary.

We had the most fun on the seesaw, which is surprising considering our relative sizes. They don't call him Bigfoot for nothing; he's big *everything*. I only weigh 124 lbs, but Bigfoot taught me that the key to balancing was in locating the fulcrum at the right spot. If Bigfoot and I sat on either end of the 12-ft seesaw, where did we put the fulcrum so we could balance?

ABOUT SEESAWS: The left weight is two times as heavy as the right weight. To balance the seesaw, the lighter weight has to be placed twice as far from the fulcrum as the heavier weight.

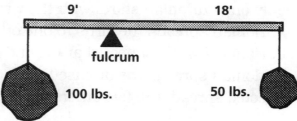

Choose one:

1. Write a short scene in which a student encounters the Loch Ness Monster.
2. Suppose the narrator invited Bigfoot over for supper. Write the dialogue that would transpire during the meal.
3. Prepare to act out one of the two choices above.

Planetary Health Crisis

Curiosity may have killed the cat, but generosity is what endangers the entire civilization of the small planet of Purlonia. Sharing food has long been a sign of friendship in the Purlonian culture. It is common for friends to bite from the same fruit or eat from the same dish, but scientists now believe that this custom is responsible for the recent spread of the deadly billow virus.

Billow virus remains dormant in its victim for 10 years but then becomes active and causes Billow Nerve Syndrome (BNS), a fatal disease in which the victim's nervous system is slowly dissolved. The dormant period is dangerous because infected Purlonians can spread the disease through the ten-year dormancy without even realizing they're carrying it.

Let's look at how rapid the spread of the billow virus can be: Suppose only one Purlonian starts with the virus and each year every infected Purlonian spreads the virus to one other Purlonian. How many Purlonians will be infected at the end of 10 years? What if each infected Purlonian spreads the disease to two others each year? What if those infected spread it to five others each year?

Choose one:

1. Perhaps the billow virus is actually an alien trying to take over the planet of Purlonia. Write the Master Plan for this takeover, or draw a meeting of the Billow leaders conducting a strategy meeting.

Flying Zorks of Migork

The Zorks of Migork are known for their blue hair
and for being inventors most extraordinaire.
They invented mighoppers and dwendles and stwees
and mini-skateboards to be ridden by fleas.
They made the cartoogin and electric shoelace,
but their most famous invention is the Flying Smipsmace.

A Smipsmace is made by four machines in a row,
with gears that are oiled with Migorkian snow.
First is the meznorter making 22 each hour,
next the grank granking 16 at full power.
Only 13 per hour then go through the haftep,
then 7 per hour from the blemp, the last step.
The machines are expensive—they cost lots of money,
and waste to a Zork is not a bit funny.

Design a factory using only fourteen machines,
that produces Smipsmaces at a rate seldom seen.
After choosing the machines that your factory will use,
calculate the hourly production, and report it as news.

Choose one:
1. Draw a Zork using a Flying Smipsmace.
2. Draw a diagram illustrating a four-step manufacturing process.
3. Write your own rhyming story about a Migorkian dessert, sport, or tourist attraction.
4. Draw Migork and write directions for getting there from Earth.

Czech Mate

My friend Jarda earns college money by betting on chess games with his parents, who were both national chess champions in the Czech Republic where they grew up. I once got so confused playing Jarda that I asked him which direction the Pope could move. He smiled and asked me if I meant the bishop. He also had to remind me that a prawn was a shrimp, not a chess piece. If I depended on chess bets for my income, I'd end up putting my parents through college rather than vice versa.

Here's how Jarda's system works: He earns $120 a month as a waiter, and he bets 15% of this income on chess games with his dad and only 10% on games with his mom. (She's the better player and beats Jarda 3/5 of the time—3 times as often as her husband does.) Jarda uses 25% of his income for spending money and 20% on car expenses. He puts the rest of his money, plus his chess winnings, into his savings account.

What percentage of Jarda's savings come from chess games? What is his monthly profit from playing chess with both parents?

Choose one:
1. Draw your partner as a chess piece.
2. Rename and draw a set of chess pieces.

Drilling for Dollars

Heather's father is an engineer for a company that makes appliances. He wants Heather to be an engineer, too, so he keeps bringing her math challenges from his job. Heather would rather work as a journalist for a newspaper. Although she has no interest in becoming an engineer, she tries all of her dad's challenges because he doubles her allowance for the week whenever she gets one right.

This week's challenge is to reduce the amount of time that an automatic drilling machine takes to drill five holes in a plastic part. Right now, the computer-controlled drill follows path ABCEDA. Her dad says he's been asked to change the path to reduce the total distance the drill travels by at least 10%. By reducing the drilling time, the company will be able to complete more parts per hour. Can you solve Heather's challenge?

	E	D	C	B
A	85	111	96	116
B	53	70	96	
C	45	34		
D	32			

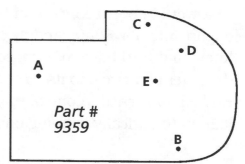

Part #9359

Choose one:

1. Draw the device that Part #9359 is a part of.
2. Draw a drilling machine that has escaped from the factory.
3. Write a letter from Heather to her father begging him to stop giving challenges.

Speeds & Sprockets

The front sprocket of a 3-speed bike is 6" in diameter. The diameters of the back sprockets for the 1st, 2nd, and 3rd speeds are 4", 3", and 2", respectively. The diameter of the back wheel is 25". For each speed, calculate how many times the back wheel will turn and how far the bike will move when the pedals move around once. Solutions must include diagrams and explanations. All correct solutions will be entered in a random drawing, and three winners will be chosen. (Ages 10-15)

Eddie nearly passed out when he saw this sign in the bike shop window. After cutting lawns for three months, he still hadn't saved enough for a mountain bike—although he had acquired grass stains that would never come out of his skin. The bike contest was a golden opportunity for Eddie, and he had some ideas about the problem. He knew that he'd have to learn something about π and how it related the diameter of a circle to its circumference. By the end of the week, Eddie had turned in one of the only two correct solutions to the problem, automatically winning one of the bikes. Can you do it?

Spice It Up!

Design and draw one of the following bikes:
- one that can travel where bikes don't usually travel
- one that is mega-comfortable to ride
- one that would be embarrassing to ride
- one that would make people laugh

Kaely's CAT Dreams

While most kids have dreams about magic places and family pets, five-year-old Kaely Curtis has dreams about medical procedures. In one week of dreams alone, Kaely performed two heart transplants, delivered a set of quintuplets, and invented a new procedure for removing warts.

In one of her more bizarre dreams, Kaely was responsible for scheduling patients for CAT scans in a large hospital. (A CAT scan is similar to a 3-dimensional x-ray.) Kaely had to schedule each of the 9 patients in the diagram below. The doctors indicated how quickly they needed each scan by assigning priority numbers (P1=highest priority, and so on). Other factors played a role in determining the best schedule for the scans. For example, the hospital's two scanners have to be set up differently for different tests, so it's sometimes advantageous to schedule groups of similar scans together. (The arrows in the diagram indicate that P5 should be done before P2 or P6; scans P4, P7, P8, and P9 could be done in any order; and so on.)

Create two different schedules for the use of the scanners, and compare the advantages and disadvantages of your schedules.

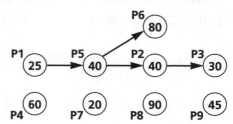

Choose one:

1. Describe or illustrate another dream that would be very unusual for a five year old.
2. Draw a cat being scanned.

Toothpaste in the Basement

Even cute names like "cinnamint" don't hide the fact that most tooth-pastes taste yucky, Elana thought. Elana decided to invent a tooth-paste that people would really like. So she created two new toothpaste flavors: Candy Madness and Maple Sugar Supreme.

She mixes the toothpastes in large tanks in her basement after school. Both flavors are made from only four ingredients, which we'll call A, B, C, and D to preserve Elana's trade secrets. Ingredients A, B, and D are pumped into Tank 1 and mixed to make Candy Madness, which requires 2 gallons of B and 3 gallons of D for every gallon of A. Two-thirds of this mixture are drained and packaged, but one-third is pumped into Tank 2 where it is mixed with other ingredients to make Maple Sugar Supreme. This second recipe requires three times the amount of A used in Candy Madness, and it is flavored with 2 gallons of C for every 3 gallons of A.

If Elana's process produces 21 gallons of Maple Sugar Supreme per hour, how many gallons of Candy Madness are produced per hour?

Spice It Up!

Choose one:
1. Make up your own tooth paste recipe.
2. Design the label for one of Elana's toothpastes.
3. List 10 new toothpaste flavors that you'd love to use.

More Than Just
ANSWERS

5

WHAT'S IN A SOLUTION?

This chapter contains annotated solutions to the 40 problems in Chapters 3 and 4. Below is a description of the purpose of each of the side-column features found on the solution pages.

More Than One Approach: Variation in methods for solving problems should be encouraged. Annotations to the solutions describe other ways that students might approach the problems. Reading these descriptions will prepare you to guide your students and provide you with variations to share in discussions.

A Gentle Reminder: General tips for managing problem-solving work are offered on pages 12-14 in Chapter 2. In the solutions, these points are reiterated and applied to the specifics of the problems.

Leading Questions: These imaginary quotes model ways to ask students questions that make them aware of the progress they have already made and move them closer to a solution without giving away too much information. Leading questions are discussed in detail on pages 21-25 in Chapter 2.

An Extra Helping: These notes provide ideas for problem extensions that can be offered to advanced students or to the whole class during discussions.

Conversation Piece: These notes provide food for thought about related math topics or real-world applications. You can use them to stimulate your own thoughts or to enrich classroom discussion.

AWARDS

The work in this book is challenging. Give students ample praise for any successes they have. The following page is a certificate you can give students at the end of a problem-solving unit. In addition, students should be able to do or receive something concrete after finishing each problem. One suggestion is to have students add a noodle to a class string of macaroni after completing each solution. A macaroni string of a certain length can be traded in for an agreed-upon class reward.

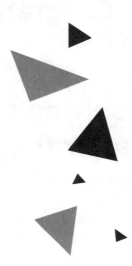

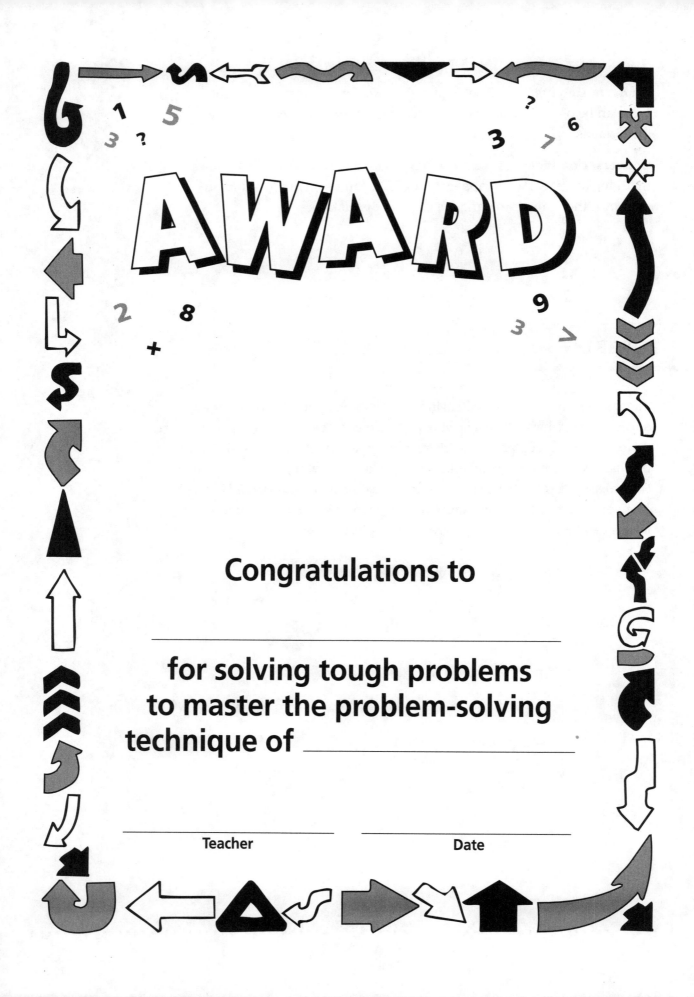

AWARD

Congratulations to

_____

for solving tough problems
to master the problem-solving
technique of _____

_____ _____
Teacher   Date

A Mouse in the House

▲▲▲▲▲▲▲▲▲▲▲▲▲▲▲▲▲▲▲▲▲▲▲

Facts: 1. room = 12' x 15'
2. tiles = 9" x 9"
3. checkerboard pattern on the floor—half the tiles have Mickey

One Approach: For many students the tricky part of the problem is that the tile dimensions are in inches and the room dimensions are in feet. Some students may convert the room dimensions to inches and then show each inch on their diagram. If this is the method they choose, let them follow it through, even though it may be a bit cumbersome. Other students may notice that every four 9" tiles cover 3'. The room can be broken down into 3' by 3' sections. The solution shown follows this line of reasoning.

	3 ft. = 4 tiles	6 ft. = 8 tiles	9 ft. = 12 tiles	12 ft. = 16 tiles	15 ft. = 20 tiles
3 ft. = 4 tiles					
6 ft. = 8 tiles					
9 ft. = 12 tiles					
12 ft. = 16 tiles					

Step 1: Since the tiles are 9" across, it takes four of them to make 36" which is 3"

Step 2: Across the room there are 5 groups of tiles. (This can be found from the diagram of from dividing 15' by 3" per group.)

Step 3: 5 groups of tiles across x 4 tiles in each group = 20 tiles across.

Step 4: Similarly, there are 16 tiles running vertically.

Step 5: 20 tiles across x 16 tiles down = 320 tiles total.

Step 6: Only half the tiles have Mickey. 320 ÷ 2 = 160 Mickey tiles.

▲ Anna will need 160 Mickey Mouse tiles.

Challenge: 160 tiles ÷ 12 = 13.33 dozen, which must be rounded up to 14 dozen. The cost for these tiles is 14 x $24.95 per dozen = $349.30.

MORE THAN ONE APPROACH

Students may find different ways to group the tiles. Here are two examples:

1. Divide the floor into 3' by 3' sections, each containing 16 tiles. The drawing will show there are 20 sections (5 across and 4 vertically).

2. Figure out the room dimensions in inches and divide the length along each side of the room by 9". (This can be done graphically or with division.) 180" ÷ 9" per tile = 20 tiles across. 144" ÷ 9" per tile = 16 tiles vertically.

A GENTLE REMINDER

By all means, let students use calculators for these problems. The focus is on learning and practicing techniques for solving problems, not on practicing computation. Although estimation skills are very handy for problem solving, students may get bogged down in multiplication and long division algorithms, taking their attention away from the real problem.

LEADING QUESTIONS

"I can see from your calculations that you got 320 for an answer. 320 what? Have you checked this answer with your facts to make sure you've taken everything into consideration?"

AN EXTRA HELPING

Try making up a problem in which the dimensions of the room are not easily divisible by the dimensions of the tile. Have students discuss their ways of handling the extra areas.

Goodbye, Spy!

Facts:
1. Houses were 32 feet apart.
2. Windows were 15 feet off the ground.
3. Cable was buried in a 1-ft deep trench.
4. Wire was needed for bedrooms, which are 12 ft x 12 ft.

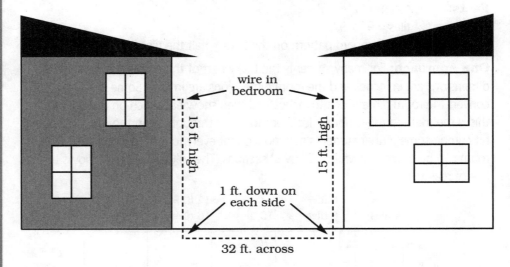

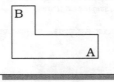
One Approach: The first part of this problem requires only a simple diagram (although details may be added for fun). The only tricky part is figuring how much wire should be allowed for each bedroom, and this figure will vary depending on the assumptions and decisions that an individual student makes.

Step 1: Draw a diagram of the path the wire will take, and label the distance on each part of the path.

Step 2: In this solution, enough wire will be put into each bedroom so it can come through the window in one wall, go around the outside edge of the bedroom, and get hooked up to an intercom on the opposite wall. The amount needed turns out to be 24 feet of wire per bedroom.

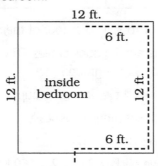

Step 3: Add together all the lengths.

24 ft + 15 ft + 1 ft + 32 ft + 1 ft + 15 ft + 24 ft = 112 ft

▲ Everett should buy 112 feet of wire.

Bushes That Bite

▲▲▲▲▲▲▲▲▲▲▲▲▲▲▲▲▲▲

Facts:
1. Bushes are 2' across.
2. 1 foot of space is needed between bushes.
3. driveway = 32' long
4. Bushes are on both sides of driveway.

One Approach: Each bush requires 2' plus another 1' of space. Dividing the 32' length of the driveway by 3' per bush indicates that a little more than 10 bushes will fit on one side of the driveway. The drawing shown helps to clarify what will happen with the extra space at the end.

Step 1: Draw the first bush at the end of the driveway. The inside edge of the bush will be 2' from the driveway.

Step 2: Draw the second bush 1' away from the first. The inside edge of this bush will be 3' from the inside edge of the first, which is 5' from the end of the driveway.

Step 3: Keep adding bushes until you notice that each bush adds another 3' onto the total distance from the end of the driveway. Now, as you add bushes, you can work faster by counting by 3s.

Step 4: The final bush ends at the 32' mark, which is the length of the driveway.

Step 5: There are 11 bushes, but the facts say that there should be bushes on both sides of the driveway. 2 x 11 = 22 bushes.

▲ Mrs. Ternavasio should order 22 barberry bushes.

end of driveway

2 ft.

1 ft. between

5 ft.

8 ft.

11 ft.

14 ft.

17 ft.

20 ft.

23 ft.

26 ft.

29 ft.

32 ft.

MORE THAN ONE APPROACH

Some students may choose to leave space at one or both ends of the driveway for design purposes. Thus a different number of bushes will be needed. These solutions are also correct; the important part is that the students make a drawing to plan where the bushes will go.

A GENTLE REMINDER

The facts should be a quick way to gather information needed to solve the problem. They can be written in a shorthand manner to conserve time, but units of measure and important ideas should be included.

LEADING QUESTIONS

"I see that you're stuck. Are you not sure where to begin? I suggest you just use your facts to draw the first two bushes. Maybe that will lead you to the next step."

AN EXTRA HELPING

Many variations of this problem can be posed by changing the garden shape or the size of the plants.

1. Create a garden that is rectangular, triangular, round, oval, or irregularly shaped.

2. Specify several different plants, each with a different dimension.

As the specifications become more complex, the solutions will become more varied and will include aesthetic considerations.

Park-o-Mania

▲▲▲▲▲▲▲▲▲▲▲▲▲▲▲▲

Facts: 1. Two stores are 25 yards apart.
2. parking lot to stores = 10 yd wide
3. Walk from car, to one store, to the other, and to the car.

One Approach: Those with strong math backgrounds may be all ready to jump right in with the Pythagorean theorem, trigonometry, or calculus, but hold on – your students probably aren't ready yet. Using a scale drawing with a trial-and-error approach can help.

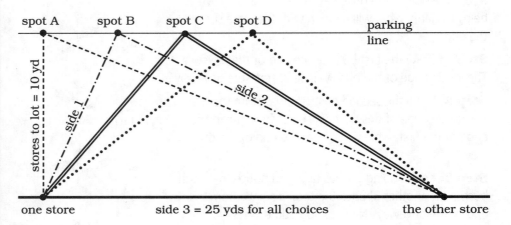

Step 1: Draw a scale diagram to show the stores and the parking lot. The diagram above was originally drawn on a scale of 1 cm = 1 yd. Larger scales will lead to greater accuracy.

Step 2: Locate several possible parking spaces. Only spaces on the left side have been tested, because they are geometrically equivalent to spaces on the right side.

Step 3: The total walking distance for any path is Side 1 + Side 2 + Side 3. The third side will always be the same because it is the 25 yards between the stores, so it has not been included in the calculations.

Step 4: Add Side 1 and Side 2 for the alternatives to find the shortest path. In the diagram above, Path A = 37 yd, Path B = 33.8 yd, Path C = 32.1 yd and Path D = 32 yd.

▲ Path D is the shortest. The best parking space is halfway between the stores. Refer to "More Than One Way."

Using the diagram shown, you can also derive an equation for the sums of the squares of the sides of the walking triangle:

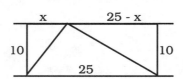

$$S = 2x^2 - 50x + 1450$$

You vary x and calculate values for S. You can graph S versus x, or you can use derivatives. Each will lead to S being minimized when $x = 12.5$ yd., or half the distance between the stores.

Executive Blocks

▲▲▲▲▲▲▲▲▲▲▲▲▲▲▲▲▲

Facts: 1. original tower = 2 in. wide x 2 in. long x 16 in. tall
2. Blocks are 1-inch cubes.
3. New tower uses same number of blocks.
4. All three dimensions of new tower are identical.

One Approach: This problem lends itself perfectly to the use of blocks. If you can, make them available to your students. Many students will not automatically be able to calculate the number of blocks in a tower, even if they have previously memorized a formula for the volume of a rectangular solid. This solution shows how the problem might be solved by a student without blocks.

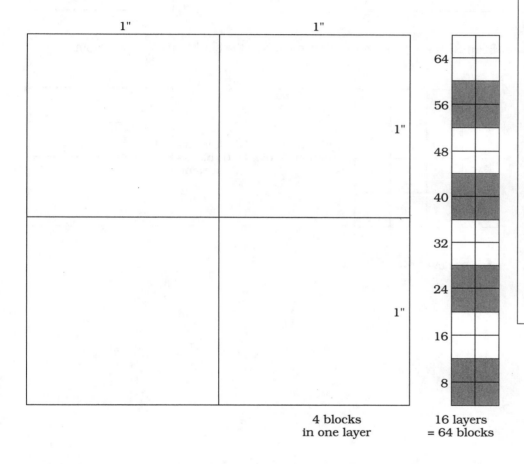

4 blocks
in one layer

16 layers
= 64 blocks

A GENTLE REMINDER

Do your students get an opportunity to share their creations from Spice It Up? Sharing artwork and writing after going over a problem or at the end of class will give students the audience they crave.

LEADING QUESTIONS

"How many blocks were in the original tower? For the new tower, maybe you can just start with the first layer. What does the last fact tell you about the shape of the first layer?"

AN EXTRA HELPING

1. Have the students see how many different towers they can make from the 64 blocks. The towers can be of any height or width but must be rectangular solids. How many of them appear square when viewed from above?
2. Can the same blocks be used to construct a building that has exactly 8 sides? How many ways can this be done? How about a building with exactly 10 sides?

Step 1: Draw the original tower according to the facts given, starting with the first layer. There are 4 blocks in the first layer. In every two layers, there are 8 blocks. The drawing on the right shows the tower built in groups of 8 blocks until there are 16 layers. This tower has 64 blocks.

Step 2: The new tower will also have 64 blocks, and all three dimensions will be the same. Therefore, the bottom layer (defined by two of these dimensions) will be a square. Try a 3 in. x 3 in. square:

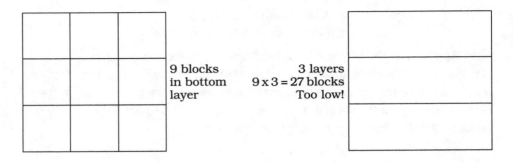

9 blocks
in bottom
layer

3 layers
9 x 3 = 27 blocks
Too low!

Step 3: The 3 x 3 x 3 tower does not use all the blocks. Try a 4 x 4 bottom:

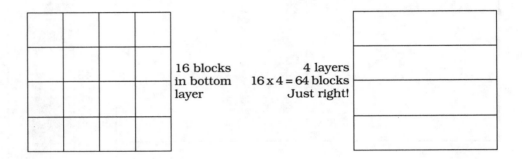

16 blocks
in bottom
layer

4 layers
16 x 4 = 64 blocks
Just right!

▲ The new tower is 4 in. x 4 in. x 4 in.

Doodles of Poodles
▲▲▲▲▲▲▲▲▲▲▲▲▲▲▲▲▲▲▲▲▲▲

Facts:
1. 3" of space at bottom of page
2. page = 8 ½" wide
3. 1" margin on each side
4. 4 equal frames

One Approach: The straightforward approach that a student might take is to divide the 6 ½ in. in the middle by 4. However, there are many ways to divide the space into four equal sections without using a division algorithm. One method, in which the space is cut in half twice, is shown below.

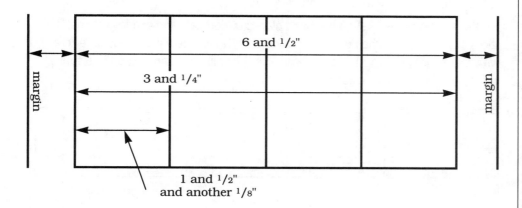

Step 1: Find out how much room there is for the frames. With 1 inch on either side for the borders, there are 6 ½ inches left in the middle.

Step 2: Divide the middle section in half. Half of the 6 inches is 3 inches, and half of ½ inches is ¼ inches. Each of the new pieces is 3 ¼ in. wide.

Step 3: Divide each of the two new sections in half. Half of 3 inches is 1 ½ inches, and half of ¼ inches is ⅛ inches.

Step 4: Put together the 1 ½ in. piece with the ⅛ in. piece to make a 1 ⅝ inch frame.

▲ Each frame should be 1 ⅝ inches wide.

Applications: Students should be able to use the skill of dividing spaces into equal sections in other creations, such as, calendars, greeting cards, brochures, gameboards, comic books, advertisements, report covers, posters, and displays. Use of a straight edge and a ruler can give these products a sharp look. As you go through the school year, look for opportunities to show students how to practice this skill.

MORE THAN ONE APPROACH

1. To find equal sections, someone may count eighths along the ruler (maybe without even knowing that these are eighths). There are 52 eighths, which can be divided into four equal groups of 13 eighths each.

2. It is possible to divide the sections in half without even using numbers. Place a piece of paper along the bottom line and mark the endpoints of the section you want to divide. Fold the paper in half so the endpoints meet. Ta-da! The distance between the fold and the endpoints is half the length of the original line.

A GENTLE REMINDER

Provide at least one place in the room where a pair of students can confer about a problem, even during quiet periods. Model how these conferences can be used for sharing hints and ideas, not for giving answers.

LEADING QUESTIONS

"You've got the facts down, but beyond that your paper seems to be blank. You've got to start somewhere. Tell me what you have to draw. Just ignore all the dimensions for a minute and show me what that might look like. Now, which dimension do you have to figure out? Put the facts on the drawing that you made and see if that leads you anywhere."

AN EXTRA HELPING

Challenge the students to divide a 7 ½ inch line into 3, 4, 5, and 6 equal sections. Have some students try it with a ruler, and have others try it without a measuring device.

Bye, Bye, Bunnies!

Facts:
1. Records are 12 in. (1 ft) across.
2. jukebox: 30 in. wide x 42 in. tall
3. She collected 100 records.
4. Wall is 12 ft 6 in. wide x 8 ft high.
5. Window is 2 ft wide x 30 in. tall.
6. Window is 20 in. from ceiling and 4 ft from left side.

One Approach: The complications of this problem may lead to variation and panic. First, students' answers will vary depending on decisions they make about the placement of the jukebox and the design of the room. The details may seem intimidating at first, but if students are encouraged to add the facts to the drawing, one by one, the problem will unwind readily.

For this solution, the jukebox has been placed underneath the window so that it sticks out 6 inches to the right of the window. This is where it will least interfere with the record pattern. The open space on the wall has been divided into four areas, and the records for each have been planned.

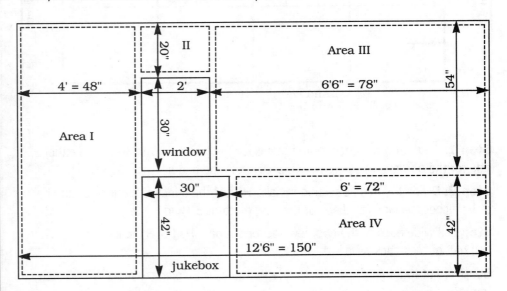

Step 1: After locating the jukebox, figure out the missing dimensions in the room and add them to the diagram.

Step 2: Divide the blank space into four areas and figure out how many records will go in each.

Area I: 4 ft wide x 8 ft high	4 x 8 = 32 records
Area II: 2 ft wide x 20 ft high	2 x 1 = 2 records
Area III: 6 ft 6 in. wide x 54 in. high	6 x 4 = 24 records
Area IV: 6 ft wide x 42 in. high	6 x 3 = 18 records

Step 3: Add together the records for each area. 32 + 2 + 24 + 18 = 76

▲ With this plan, Denise will use 76 records.

A Treat for the Feet

▲▲▲▲▲▲▲▲▲▲▲▲▲▲▲▲▲▲▲▲▲

Facts: 1. Room dimensions are shown below.
2. carpeting — 12' wide rolls
3. not too many seams

One Approach: If you don't want to use scale rolls of carpeting (as described in "More Than One Approach"), you can experiment with different ways of cutting and laying out the carpeting on a drawing. This solution shows only one way to cut the pieces. There are other ways that will work, and some will waste less square footage. The placement of seams is an economic and an aesthetic decision, so there is no "best" solution. Rather, there are only good solutions.

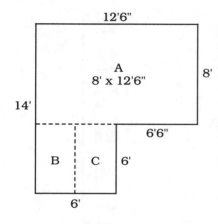
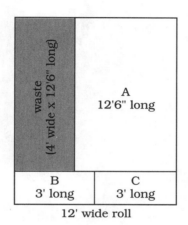

Step 1: Fill in the missing dimensions on the room diagram. At first, it looks as if dimensions are missing on the problem sheet, but all the dimensions can easily be calculated from the values given.

Step 2: Mark off where the seams *might* go. Keep in mind that no piece of carpeting can be more than 12' wide. The room on the left has been divided into sections A, B, and C.

Step 3: Draw a diagram like the one on the right, showing a 12' wide piece of carpeting. On this diagram, "cut" appropriate lengths to match the pieces on the room diagram.

Step 4: From the finished carpeting diagram, determine the total length of 12 foot carpeting needed: 12' 6" + 3' = 15' 6"

Step 5: (not shown) Try another plan. Follow the same steps to show where the seams would go and how the pieces would be cut.

Step 6: Consider the lengths and placements of the seams and the amounts of wasted carpeting, and choose which plan you're going to use.

▲ According to the plan shown, Denise will need to buy 15' 6" of black carpeting.

MORE THAN ONE APPROACH

This problem can also be solved with a scale diagram. Have students make scale drawings of the room. (1 cm = 1 ft works well.) Provide 12-cm wide strips of paper, representing the 12' wide roll of carpeting. Students can cut out pieces from the "roll" and cover their scale rooms. See how many different ways the floor can be covered. Which ways minimize the amount of wasted carpet? Which solutions don't require seams that are too numerous or too complicated?

A GENTLE REMINDER

Don't be fooled into thinking that problems like this one are too hard. If students just look at the problems and think about them, they'll find them very difficult and get discouraged. However, if they follow the first steps of gathering the facts and drawing a picture, the steps to a solution will unfold.

LEADING QUESTIONS

"You've done a great job of sketching the room and the dimensions. You even figured out the numbers that were missing. Does this dotted line across the middle show where one section of carpeting will end? If you drew a piece of 12' wide carpeting, could you then start drawing pieces on it to match the pieces you've drawn on the room?"

Fine Feathered Friend?

Facts:
1. Kid gets 3-block headstart.
2. Store is 6 blocks east and 8 blocks north.
3. person zigzags east and north, bird flies straight
4. Both travel at same speed.

One Approach: Methods of solving this problem using equations and calculations will be left for "More Than One Approach." Here is a simple diagram solution.

MORE THAN ONE APPROACH

There are several methods available to those who know a little about triangles. These methods aren't necessarily better.

1. Baldwin traveled the hypotenuse of a right triangle, and the person traveled both legs. Use the Pythagorean theorem to calculate the length of Baldwin's trip.

$$Baldwin = \sqrt{6^2 + 8^2}$$

2. The ratio of the sides of the triangle is 3:4:5. Doubling these numbers but keeping the ratios the same gives a triangle with sides that are 6:8:10. The person walked the 6-block and 8-block sides, and Baldwin flew the 10-block side.

A GENTLE REMINDER

Although it is important to let students solve a problem using their own methods, it is helpful to share other ways of viewing the problem later. Sharing can highlight other interesting approaches. For example, in this problem you can show the Pythagorean theorem because it's an interesting approach—not a better approach.

LEADING QUESTIONS

"I like the details in your drawing, especially this little guy right here. Your blocks look even. Did you use a ruler? How wide is each block on the ruler? Okay, then, which way did Baldwin go? Can you use your ruler to figure out that distance, too?

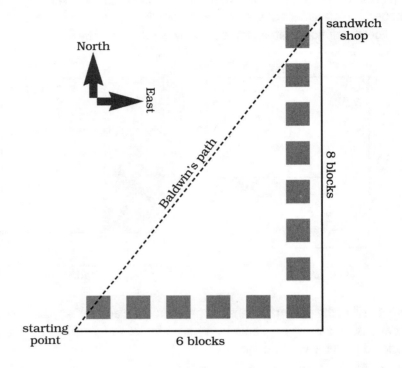

Step 1: Make a scale drawing of the paths that the bird and the person followed. A scale of 1 cm = 1 block was used for the diagram shown.

Step 2: Measure the length of Baldwin's path on the diagram. From above, Baldwin's path = 10 cm, which stands for 10 blocks.

Step 3: The person had to travel a total of 14 blocks, but he or she had a 3-block headstart. That means that the race distance for the person was 14 - 3 = 11 blocks.

▲ Since they traveled at the same speed, Baldwin must have finished 1 block ahead of the person.

Cupcake Clutter

▲▲▲▲▲▲▲▲▲▲▲▲▲▲▲

Facts:
1. Boxes are 18" x 31"
2. Cupcakes are 3" across the top and 2" across the bottom.
3. 420 cupcakes altogether

One Approach: This solution is based on a quick and simple diagram that shows the relationship between the cupcakes and the box. A student may find the number of cupcakes along one edge by drawing them and adding up 3s or by dividing.

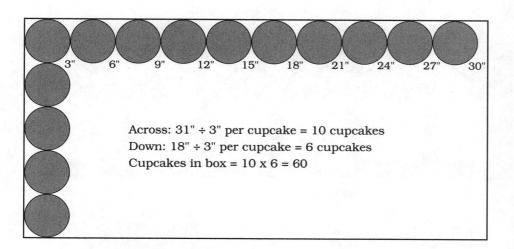

Across: 31" ÷ 3" per cupcake = 10 cupcakes
Down: 18" ÷ 3" per cupcake = 6 cupcakes
Cupcakes in box = 10 x 6 = 60

Step 1: Draw the box and find out how many cupcakes are along each edge. From this information, calculate the number of cupcakes in one box. There are 60 cupcakes in one box.

Step 2: Figure out the number of boxes needed. 420 ÷ 60 = 7 boxes.

▲ Eva will need 7 boxes to hold all the cupcakes.

Challenge: If every other cupcake is turned upside-down, the cupcakes take up less space. The diagram shows that 12 cupcakes can be packed along the 31" edge of the box.

total length = 30.5"

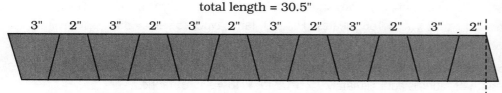

The 1 inch difference between the two cupcake dimensions is split between the two sides of the cupcake. This means there is a 0.5 inch overhang at the right edge of the cupcake row.

Similarly, 7 cupcakes will fit along the 18" edge. In one box, Eva could pack 84 cupcakes. Therefore, she would need only 5 boxes—but what a mess it would be!

MORE THAN ONE APPROACH

Students can successfully solve this problem without using multiplication or division. For Step 2, a student could draw rectangles to represent boxes and write 60 under each. Boxes could be added until the total number of cupcakes reached 420. This method would be perfectly acceptable. Later you could demonstrate how division could be used as a shortcut for dividing the cupcakes among the boxes. If students are sharing solutions, hopefully these hints will be passed from one student to another.

A GENTLE REMINDER

Do you provide a combination of quiet time and time for conversation about the problems? Students—especially those who are introverted in their learning styles—need quiet time to concentrate on their work. Students also need time to share insights and clues. For students who are extroverted in their learning styles, this is essential. Introverted and extroverted students benefit from a combination of these two work climates.

LEADING QUESTIONS

"So you think there are 60 cupcakes in one box. How many would there be in two boxes? Can you keep going like that until you have enough boxes to hold all the cupcakes?"

T.J. in Fabricland

Facts:
1. finished quilt = 72" x 78"
2. made from 6" x 6" squares
3. 4 different types of fabric
4. cut out squares with 1/4" borders
5. fabric in 45" widths

One Approach: Diagrams can be used to help visualize each step of this problem. There is not one exact answer because estimates are made along the way. Instead, look for reasonable answers and appropriate explanations.

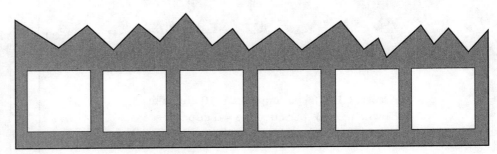

45" wide fabric: 6 squares fit across

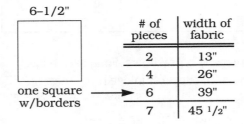

# of pieces	width of fabric
2	13"
4	26"
6	39"
7	45 1/2"

6–1/2"

one square w/borders →

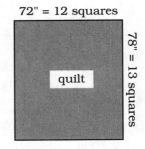

72" = 12 squares

78" = 13 squares

quilt

Step 1: Figure out how many squares will fit across the width of the fabric. First, draw the square with its border to show that it is 6 1/2" wide. The solution follows a trial-and-error approach to determine that 6 squares fit across the fabric.

Step 2: Figure out how many squares are needed for each type of fabric. The quilt will require 12 x 13 = 156 squares. For each fabric type, 156 ÷ 4 = 39 squares will be needed.

Step 3: 39 squares ÷ 6 squares per row ≈ 7 rows of squares needed. The total length of fabric is approximately 7 x 6 1/2 in. ≈ 46-49 in. of fabric.

▲ T.J. will need about 50 inches of each fabric.

CHALLENGE: He'll need approximately 1 1/2 yd of each fabric. Total cost ≈ $20.00.

MORE THAN ONE APPROACH

Some students may be able to use division to figure out how many squares will fit across the fabric, while others may figure out the number of squares along the edges of the quilt by using drawings.

Graphical and computational methods are both valid. Alternative approaches give students the power to figure things out before they're able to select and use the appropriate computational algorithm. Encouraging these techniques is more appropriate to their stage of development and valuable to their self-esteem than insisting they memorize specific procedures for specific types of problems.

LEADING QUESTIONS

"I see you've already figured out the width of one of the squares. Why don't you draw a section of the fabric to show how wide it is? Now, how many squares do you think will fit across? Show me, please."

AN EXTRA HELPING

This problem can be turned into a real-life project. Students could plan the materials and then sew together a patchwork wall-hanging. Perhaps each student could decorate a square and add it to the class or school quilt.

Look for opportunities to incorporate planning and measuring of materials into other student projects.

Emma's Dilemma

▲▲▲▲▲▲▲▲▲▲▲▲▲▲▲▲▲▲

Facts:
1. Each person had 64 blocks.
2. straight towers, square from above
3. 5 sides painted, not bottoms
4. Sammy's tower = 257 sides
5. narrator's tower = 96 sides

One Approach: This problem is wonderful to work out with a set of cubes. If you don't have any, find a primary teacher who can lend them to you. Following is a two-dimensional explanation.

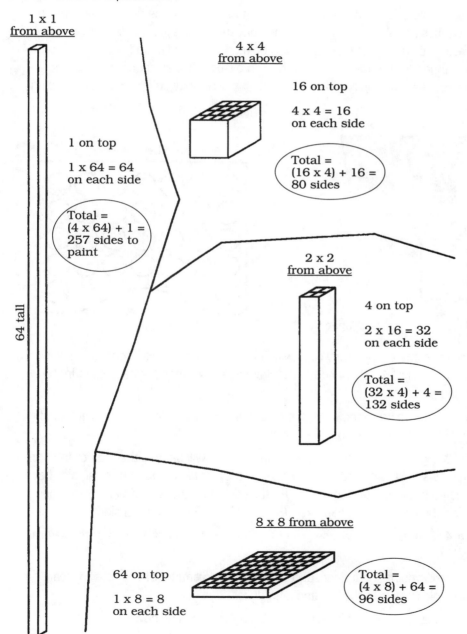

1 x 1
from above

1 on top

1 x 64 = 64
on each side

Total =
(4 x 64) + 1 =
257 sides to
paint

64 tall

4 x 4
from above

16 on top

4 x 4 = 16
on each side

Total =
(16 x 4) + 16 =
80 sides

2 x 2
from above

4 on top

2 x 16 = 32
on each side

Total =
(32 x 4) + 4 =
132 sides

8 x 8 from above

64 on top

1 x 8 = 8
on each side

Total =
(4 x 8) + 64 =
96 sides

LEADING QUESTIONS

"What does your second fact tell you? Can you think of one possibility for the first layer of the tower? Show me with these blocks. How many blocks are there in this layer? With 64 blocks, how many layers do you think you could build? Try it."

AN EXTRA HELPING

Challenge students to build rectangular towers that have the minimum or maximum number of sides facing out. You can create even more possibilities by removing the restriction that the tower be rectangular.

CONVERSATION PIECE

A tall thin building has a much larger surface exposed to the environment than does a shorter, squatter building with an equal volume. That makes it more expensive to heat. Similarly, mittens keep your fingers warmer than gloves because they reduce the surface area exposed to the cold.

Manufacturers often design the packaging for products to minimize the amount of material required. Cylindrical cans require the least sheet metal when the diameter equals the height. Tall, thin cans and short, fat cans would use more material, making them more expensive. A spherical can would minimize the surface area even more, but it isn't practical from a manufacturing standpoint.

Better Than Babysitting

▲▲▲▲▲▲▲▲▲▲▲▲▲▲▲▲▲▲▲▲▲▲▲▲▲

Facts: 1. Refer to the diagrams in the problem for dimensions of the cups and the tray.

One Approach: Teaching students how to plan dimensions empowers them to create more detailed and better-made products in their hobbies and in their school work. Notice that the answer to this problem is a plan, not a specific matter of cups that the tray will hold. Students' plans will differ, but they should include an explanation of the assumptions made, and they should show where the holes for the cups will be located.

In this sample solution, the holes are laid out in rows with the rims of the cups just barely touching. As the diagram on the right shows, this leaves 1/2 in. of material between the cups. This tray is going to be made out of plywood, so 1/2 in. seems wide enough to give the tray strength. Some students may choose to leave more space between the cups or have every other row of holes shifted in an overlapping pattern.

MORE THAN ONE APPROACH

If you were actually to build this tray, you could cut the basic shape and then trace a cardboard template of the 3 in. cups to locate holes, which wouldn't necessarily have to be arranged in rows. Some students may choose to use this approach by making a scale drawing. All variations are valid if the students can explain their reasoning.

A GENTLE REMINDER

Taking the time to make and label drawings and to write out steps in the solution to a problem reduces the risk of introducing careless errors. Clear steps on the paper necessitate and represent clear steps in thinking.

LEADING QUESTIONS

"You've made a bunch of circles on your drawing. Are those the holes that are supposed to be cut out? How can you tell how much space there is between holes? Suppose I was going to give away my new car to the one student who made the plan that would be most helpful to me when I went to build the tray. Would you want to leave this plan as it is, or would you want to be more specific about where those holes are located?

AN EXTRA HELPING

Cut out pieces of cardboard to represent the trays, and ask the students to work in pairs or groups to locate and cut out the holes. Before they cut, have them share their methods for locating and drawing the holes.

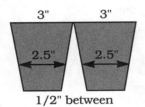

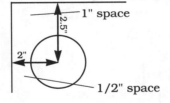

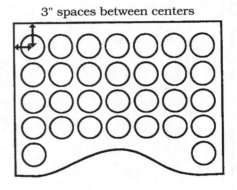

Step 1: Estimate how many cups will fit in each direction. Horizontally, $22 \div 3 \approx 7$ cups. Vertically, $14 \div 3 \approx 4$ cups. The drawing shows that 2 extra cups fit in the rounded part.

Step 2: According to the facts, the holes will be 2 1/2 in. across. The centers of the holes will be 3 in. apart.

Step 3: Figure out how much border space there will be on either side of the horizontal rows. This amount can be determined by trial and error, but it can also be calculated by subtracting the space for the cups from the total distance, and then dividing the remainder in half. $[22 - (3 \times 7)] \div 2 = 1/2$ in. on either side.

Step 4: Similarly, there will be $[14 - (3 \times 4)] \div 2 = 1$ in. at either end of the vertical rows.

Step 5: Combine the border space with half the diameter of the cups to locate the corner hole relative to the top and left edges.

▲ One possible plan for locating and cutting the holes is shown.

Matt's Metaphor Rebuttal

▲▲▲▲▲▲▲▲▲▲▲▲▲▲▲▲▲▲▲▲▲▲▲▲▲▲▲▲▲

Facts: 1. square = 10 cm x 10 cm
                2. The circle around the square is as small as possible.

One Approach: There are some simple ways to do this problem if you know a few things about triangles. These methods are described below. Here is a solution your students can follow without any prior knowledge of the relationships among the sides of right triangles.

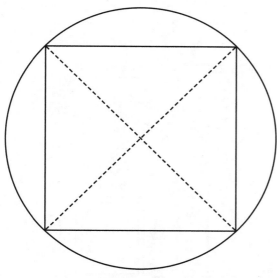

This drawing is
half the actual size.

Step 1: Draw a square with 10-cm sides.

Step 2: Experiment with circles to see how small you can make them without going into the square. Eventually you may notice that locating the center of the circle may be helpful.

Step 3: One way to locate the center is to divide the diagonal length of the square in half and then measure that distance from the corner along the diagonal. The method shown locates the center of the circle at the intersection of the two diagonals.

Step 4: Measure the diameter of the circle.

▲ The diameter of the smallest possible hole that the peg could fit through is ≈ 14.1 cm.

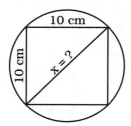

The diameter of the circle represents the third side of an isosceles triangle with two 45° angles. Some may recognize that the hypotenuse of this triangle is equal to one of the legs times √2. If not, you can use the Pythagorean theorem: $x = \sqrt{10^2 + 10^2} = \sqrt{200} \approx 14.1$ cm.

MORE THAN ONE APPROACH

Expect a variation of ± mm. Imperfect drawings and the width of the pencil lines make it hard to measure exactly. Also, some students may use a trial-and-error approach without ever locating the center of the circle. On the other hand, some students may recognize that the diameter of the smallest possible circle is also the diagonal of the square, and they may make this measurement without ever drawing any circles.

A GENTLE REMINDER

For this problem, you could share the use of the Pythagorean theorem. Some students will be interested, and some won't understand. The goal is to pique interest where you can, remembering that students will learn concepts at different times.

LEADING QUESTIONS

"You seem to be having trouble making the circles touch all four corners of the square. Is there a place that you could put the point of the compass to fix that? Where do you think that point would be? How could you be more exact?

AN EXTRA HELPING

New problems can often be created by reversing an existing problem. What's the largest square peg that you could fit into a hole with a diameter of 15 cm? Also, try changing the shape of the peg or the hole. How long are the sides of the largest regular hexagonal peg that could fit through a 15-cm round hole?

Pie Surprise

▲▲▲▲▲▲▲▲▲▲▲▲

Facts:
1. gameboard = 2' x 2'
2. 3" squares on corners
3. 8 spaces between corners
4. 1/4" borders between card and space

One Approach: Use facts, step by step, to make the drawing below.

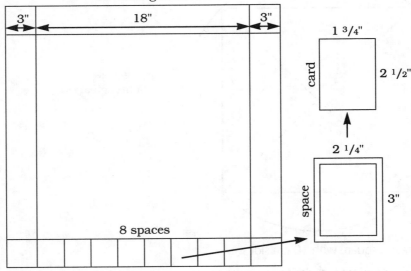

2' = 24" wide gameboard

Step 1: After the gameboard is drawn with its borders, it becomes clear that the next step is to divide the 18 inches between corners by 8 to determine the width of the 8 side-spaces. One approach is to split the 18 inches in half repeatedly until there are 8 spaces: 18" >> 9" >> 4 1/2" >> 2 1/4"

Step 2: Draw the space and show its dimensions.

Step 3: From the drawing of the space with the 1/4" border shown, you can see that the card is 1/2" smaller than the space in both directions.

Step 4: Calculate the dimensions of the card.
  Vertically: 3 - 1/2 = 2 1/2"
  Horizontally: 2 1/4 - 1/2 = 1 3/4"

▲ The side-spaces are 3" high by 2 1/4" wide.
The cards are 2 1/2" high by 1 3/4" wide.

Sister Shelter
▲▲▲▲▲▲▲▲▲▲▲▲▲▲▲

Facts: 1. block = 16" long, 8" high, and 7 1/2" wide
2. shelter = 12' long x 10' 7" wide and 6' 8" high

One way to solve it: This is another problem that can be solved with the use of blocks. Many popular building blocks are made twice as long as they are wide, approximating the proportions of the concrete blocks. Without blocks, the problem can be solved with a series of drawings similar to the one below. Figuring out the arrangement of blocks in the first layer is a great step to recommend to students who are stuck.

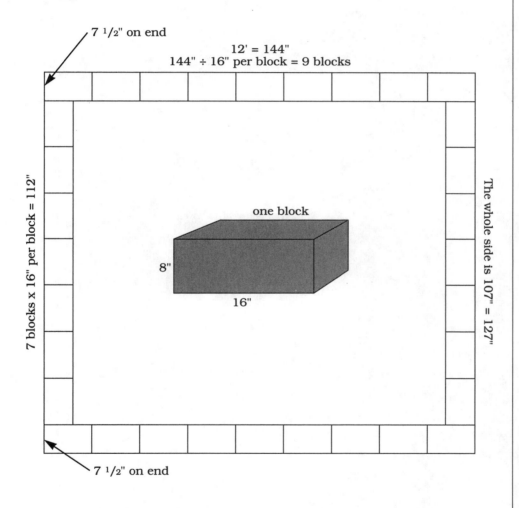

7 1/2" on end

12' = 144"
144" ÷ 16" per block = 9 blocks

7 blocks x 16" per block = 112"

one block

8"

16"

The whole side is 107" = 127"

7 1/2" on end

MORE THAN ONE APPROACH

In a real wall, the blocks would be offset in every other layer to add strength. Some answers may vary because students are taking this possible structural failure into account.

A GENTLE REMINDER

Encourage students to use calculators as a tool to solve complex problems. The students' energy should be focused on understanding and unraveling the problems. You don't want them to get bogged down with conversions and calculations done by hand – you can teach those skills at a different time.

LEADING QUESTIONS

"I can see that you're trying to divide up the 10' 7 " side into 16" blocks, and you're wondering if you can cut blocks? You can if you want to, but you don't really need to. Could you draw the corner for me first so that we can see what the blocks will look like there?"

AN EXTRA HELPING

This problem can easily be made more challenging by adding other specifications to the building. Ask students to include windows and/or doors. You can set the dimensions of these additions so they are multiples of the block dimensions, or you can specify unusual dimensions so students have to make decisions about cutting blocks.

Try making up problems with unusually shaped buildings constructed from a variety of materials.

Step 1: Draw the outline of the first layer. Label the sides in feet and in inches.

Step 2: There are 144 ÷ 16 = 9 blocks along the 12' wall.

Step 3: Figure out the number of blocks along the 10' 7 " (127") wall.

7 blocks x 16" per block = 112". The width of the two blocks at the end make up for the remaining 15".

Step 4: Counting shows there are 32 blocks in the first layer.

Step 5: Use a diagram or division to figure out that there are 10 layers in the 80" high building. 10 layers x 32 blocks per layer = 320 blocks.

▲ Carlos needs 32 blocks for each layer, or 320 blocks in all.   Making the door and window described in the challenge requires knocking out 16 blocks for the door and 4 1/2 blocks for the window.

Dream Dwelling

▲▲▲▲▲▲▲▲▲▲▲▲▲▲▲▲▲

Facts: 1. room = 14' x 20'
2. 2' 6 " door near corner
3. See problem for furniture dimensions.

One approach: Making scale pieces of furniture out of paper and then moving them around in a scale room is a popular method for solving this type of problem. The drawing below was made by sliding the furniture around not only so it fit, but also so that the arrangement made sense.   The latter is an important aspect to keep in mind.   As students share their solutions with you, ask why they chose their locations.

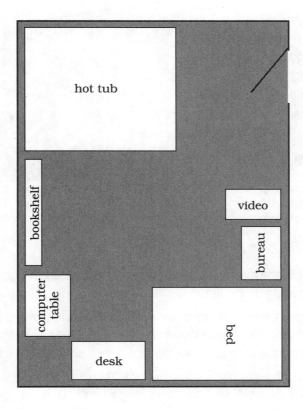

MORE THAN ONE APPROACH

Using graph paper is another excellent way to plan the arrangement of furniture. With quarter-inch or centimeter ruled paper, one square per foot is a convenient scale that makes it easy to draw the room and the furniture. Pieces can be cut out and moved, or they can be drawn and erased until a final arrangement has been chosen.

A GENTLE REMINDER

Some problems lend themselves very well to individual expression. Students will have different arrangements for the furniture, and they may add all kinds of interesting details. Perhaps they'll add furniture or build lofts, include lighting or electronic gadgetry, or build windows or trap doors.

LEADING QUESTIONS

"You're right, it all seems to fit in the room pretty easily. And look, you've got all this extra space at one end of the room. What are you planning to do with that? You can include an aviary if you want. I do have one question, though. I was wondering how you were going to open the drawers of the dresser since it's right next to your desk?"

▲ The scale used for this design was 1 cm = 1 ft. The problem said there was a door in the corner, but it didn't specify which corner.

For this arrangement, the hot tub was located in its own end of the room away from sleeping areas and anything that would be damaged by splashed water. The computer table and desk were used to create a study area. The bureau was put next to the bed, where it could be used as a night stand.

In the Doghouse

▲▲▲▲▲▲▲▲▲▲▲▲▲▲▲▲▲

Facts:
1. Plywood comes in 4' x 8' sheets.
2. House is 3' wide, 2' 6" deep with a 1' 8" square door in front.
3. Front wall is 3' high, back wall is 2' high.
4. Roof sticks out ≈ 6" on all sides.

One Approach: The following solution makes use of scale drawings and graph paper.

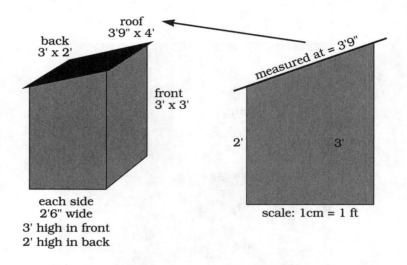

each side
2'6" wide
3' high in front
2' high in back

scale: 1cm = 1 ft

Step 1: Figure out the dimensions of the sides. These are taken from the facts and labeled in the drawing on the left.

Step 2: Figure out the dimensions of the roof. First, a scale drawing was made of one side of the doghouse. The roof was extended on both ends to account for the 6" overhang. From the scale drawing, the roof is measured at about 3 3/4', which equals 3' 9".

Step 3: On graph paper, draw blank sheets of plywood. Draw the pieces in different arrangements until you find one that works well, preferably minimizing the number of sheets needed.

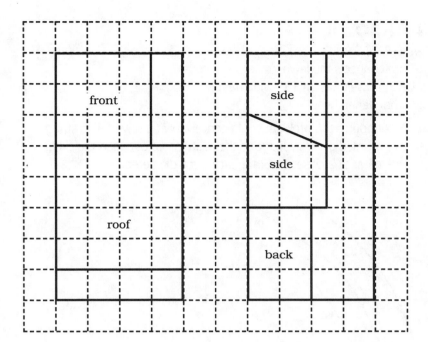

LEADING QUESTIONS

"I agree, that part's pretty tough. A lot of people have had trouble figuring out how long to make the roof along the slanted edge. Show me what the side looks like. Suppose I gave you a piece of plywood cut like that. Could you then measure the length of the slanted edge where the roof goes? I don't have any big pieces of plywood to give you, but could you use your ruler to make a smaller version of the side?"

Lazy Lawnmowing

Facts:
1. Cord connects the lawnmower to the post.
2. Lawnmower cuts an 18" wide path.
3. Paths overlap by 2".

One Approach: Although this problem could conceivably be solved with string, the solution shown is based on knowledge of the relationship between the circumference and the diameter of a circle: circumference = π x diameter.

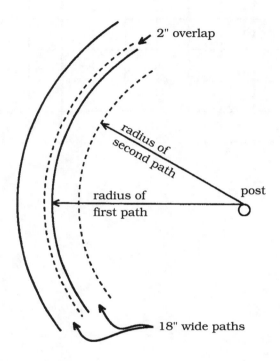

Step 1: Each trip around, the distance the lawnmower moves is equal to the length of the cord wrapped onto the post, which is the post's circumference.

Step 2: Because of the overlap, Larry wants the lawnmower to be 16" closer to the post each trip around.

Step 3: The circumference (C) of the post must be 16".
$C_{post} = 16 = π$ x diameter of post, or
diameter of post $= 16 \div π \approx 5.1" \approx 5 1/8"$

▲ Larry's lawnmower will work properly if he uses a 5 1/8" diameter post.

MORE THAN ONE APPROACH

Once a student has determined that the distance around the post must be 16", he or she could measure the diameter of a circle formed from a 16" long string.

A GENTLE REMINDER

Don't let students stay "stuck." Often students will tell you they have no idea how to solve a problem. What they really mean is that they don't see the entire path to the solution. As we walk into an unfamiliar forest, we don't necessarily see the whole path ahead of us, but as long as we keep taking steps, the path will unfold. You have to help the students to take first steps. For this problem, taking the first step means collecting the facts and then putting as much information as possible into a drawing.

LEADING QUESTIONS

"I know what we can do so you can see what's going on. Take this piece of string and use your pencil as the post. Show me how the lawnmower travels. What's happening to the string and the lawnmower as you go around? Why is the lawnmower getting closer?"

AN EXTRA HELPING

Hand a group of students a 12" LP, and ask them to determine the length of the groove. (The duration of the record and the RPM's can be used to calculate the number of turns the groove makes. The mean distance traveled by the needle in 1 turn is equal to the mean circumference of the grooved portion of the LP.)

World Problems

▲▲▲▲▲▲▲▲▲▲▲▲▲▲▲▲

Facts: 1. 15,000 globes

2. Diameter of globes = 30 cm

3. room = 12 m long x 9 m wide x 3 m high

One Approach: There are 3 different problems to solve. The first and third require filling a 3-dimensional space. The second problem, finding the size of the balls that would fit between the globes, is either a scale drawing problem or one involving the use of the Pythagorean theorem, which is shown below.

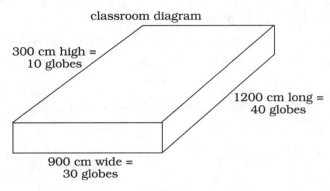

classroom diagram

300 cm high =
10 globes

1200 cm long =
40 globes

900 cm wide =
30 globes

Step 1: Find out how many globes fit along each edge of the room. For example, 30 globes can be placed across the room (900 cm ÷ 30 cm per globe). The other values are shown in the drawing above.

Step 2: Calculate the number of globes that will fit in the bottom layer: 30 x 40 = 1200 globes.

▲ 10 layers x 1200 globes per layer = 12,000 globes.

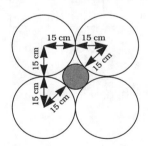

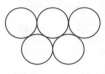

Step 3: The two legs of the right triangle are each 30 cm. Using the Pythagorean theorem:

$$\text{hypotenuse} = \sqrt{30^2 \times 30^2} \approx 42.4 \text{ cm}$$

Step 4: The diameter of the small ball equals the hypotenuse of the triangle minus twice the radius of the globes.

▲ Diameter of small ball = 42.4 - 30 = 12.4 cm.

A GENTLE REMINDER

When given a large piece of paper on which to draw, many students will use only a small fraction of the page. When drawings are used to solve a problem, this cramped spacing can cause students to miss details or clues. Encourage students to make large drawings so they can really see what is going on.

LEADING QUESTIONS

"You've drawn the circles but they don't show the size of the smaller one. Try connecting the centers of the globes. Can you get any more information from that triangle?"

AN EXTRA HELPING

Ask students to find out how many globes will fit in the first layer if they are allowed to overlap as shown below.

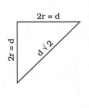

Sherlock Bothmerini

▲▲▲▲▲▲▲▲▲▲▲▲▲▲▲▲▲▲▲▲▲▲

Facts:
1. 1000 suspects in the beginning
2. Only 40% of students ate first lunch period.
3. Only 75% of first-period lunch students had hot lunch.
4. 3% of hot lunch students had access to worms.

One Approach: The solution shown does not rely on prior knowledge of percents, other than the fact that percent means "out of 100."

Step 1: Use the second fact to take 40 out of every 100 people, representing the 40% who ate during the first lunch period.

40 out of each 100 adds up to 400.

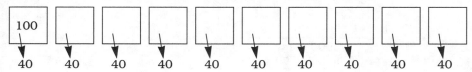

Step 2: Use the third fact to take 75 out of every 100 remaining suspects. This narrows the list to 300 suspects who had hot lunch during the first lunch period.

75 out of each 100 adds up to 300.

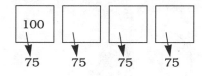

Step 3: Out of every 100 suspects left, only 3 were in the class that observed worms in science.

3 out of each 100 adds up to 9.

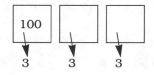

▲ The names of 9 students were given to the principal.

Infected Technology

▲▲▲▲▲▲▲▲▲▲▲▲▲▲▲▲▲▲▲▲▲▲▲

Facts:　　1. 1 computer starts with virus
　　　　　　2. Virus spreads to another computer the first day.
　　　　　　3. Every infected computer spreads virus to another computer each day.

One approach: The diagram on the right shows the spread of the virus, and the chart on the left shows the number of infected computers each day. It is not necessary to draw the spread of the virus for 10 days, because the pattern in the chart quickly shows that the number of infected computers doubles each day. With this information, the rest of the chart is filled out.

day #	infected computers
1	2
2	4
3	8
4	16
5	32
6	64
7	128
8	256
9	512
10	1024

● = original infected computer
○ = infected 1st day
△ = infected 2nd day
□ = infected 3rd day
✳ = infected 4th day

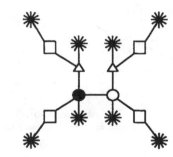

▲ 1024 computers will be infected by the end of the tenth day. After 20 days, 1,048,576 computers will have the virus.

The equation that describes how the number of infected computers relates to the number of days is:

$$N = 2^d \text{ (N = \# of infected computers, d = \# of days)}$$

What if each computer spreads the disease to *more* than one other computer each day? If C equals the number of other computers "contracting" the virus from each infected computer each day, then the general equation for the number of infected computers is:　$N = C^d$

If C = 3, then 59,049 computers will have the virus after 10 days. If C = 4, then 1,048,576 will have the virus after 10 days. Once a large number of computers from one region are infected, the spread may slow down because the pool of computers available is smaller. However, the general trend suggested by this exponential equation has serious implications in terms of controlling the spread of diseases among humans.

MORE THAN ONE APPROACH

Students will have their own styles for making a diagram for this problem. Enjoy and comment on this variety. Their organizational skills may also vary. Some will keep organized lists of the daily numbers, others will jot down notes, and others will write down nothing. This is an opportunity for you to share techniques, such as tables or lists, that they can use to organize their work.

Highly intuitive students may recognize the pattern and quickly arrive at an answer. Ask these students to explain their reasoning, pretending you don't understand and encouraging the use of a diagram to make it clearer. You will be prompting them to practice communication.

AN EXTRA HELPING

This problem is filled with a variety of wonderful opportunities.
1. Ask students to try the problem again with each infected computer spreading the virus to 2 others each day.
2. Draw a graph with your students to show the spread of the virus over time.
3. Ask students to brainstorm to list other things that grow or spread in this manner.
4. Pursue discussions of some of the topics students listed in #3. Possible discussion topics include AIDS, population growth, and the ethics of writing computer viruses.

The Clucky Winner
▲▲▲▲▲▲▲▲▲▲▲▲▲▲▲▲▲

Facts:
1. 4 kids in the family
2. Laura says there are more families with 3 of one sex and 1 of the other.
3. Alex says there are more families with 2 of each sex.

One Approach: This solution depends on a diagram that shows the birth possibilities for each of the four children.

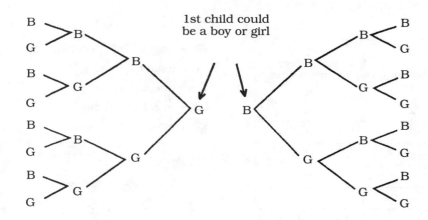

combination	how many?
4B / 0G	1
3B / 1G	4
2B / 2G	6
1B / 3G	4
0B / 4G	1

Step 1: When each child is born, it can be either a boy or a girl. Draw a branching diagram to trace all the possible combinations.

Step 2: Count the number of boys and girls in each of the 16 possible families. Tally your information in a list or a table (shown to the right).

Step 3: The table shows that there are more families with 2 children of each sex than with any other combination. But Laura didn't say which sex had 3 children. There are 4 combinations with 3 boys and a girl and 4 combinations with 3 girls and a boy.

▲ Laura was correct; there are 8 families with 3 children of one sex and 1 of the other. This answer is counter-intuitive: because there is a 50/50 chance of each child being a boy or a girl, it seems logical that families with equal numbers of boys and girls should occur most frequently.

The numbers in the right column of the table above form a row in Pascal's triangle (shown to the right). Each number in the triangle is generated by adding the two numbers above it. The rows of the triangle show the possibilities for families with different numbers of children. Find the row that corresponds to the combinations for a 4-child family. The values in the next row correspond to the combinations for a 5-child family. Try it by making a table like the one above.

Pascal's Triangle

```
              1
            1   1
          1   2   1
        1   3   3   1
      1   4   6   4   1
    1   5  10  10   5   1
  1   6  15  20  15   6   1
```

Dazed by Dollars

Facts:
1. Pays sister $1.50 for accounting.
2. Rewceives $3.75 for allowance.
3. Gets one-third of his brother's $3.75.
4. Earns $7.50 for cutting lawn.
5. Another $7.50 goes to college account for cutting lawn.
6. Pays Dad $1.75 for lawnmower expenses.
7. Pays Dad$2.25 for ruined ties.
8. Half of net income goes to college account.
9. Parents put in $1.50 for every $1.00 Mark puts in.
10. Dad puts in an additional $1.75 from lawnmower money.

One Approach: The problem asks the students to make a diagram showing the flow of money between Mark, his family members, and the college account. Here is one example of what such a diagram might look like:

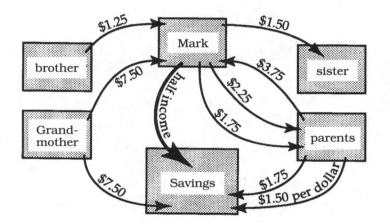

Step 1: Before figuring out Mark's income, we need to figure out how much he gets from his brother. One-third of $3.75 = $3.75 ÷ 3 = $1.25.

Step 2: Add the income: 1.25 + 7.50 + 3.75 = $12.50 per week.

Step 3: Add the expenses: 1.75 + 2.25 + 1.50 = $5.50 per week.

Step 4: Mark's net weekly income = 12.50 - 5.50 = $7.00 per week. Mark contributes half this amount ($3.50) per week into his college account.

Step 5: Mark's parents contribute $1.50 for every $1.00 Mark contributes. Their contribution = ($1.50 x 3) + $0.75 = $5.25 = $5.25 per week.

Step 6: Total Weekly Savings Increase = 7.50 + 3.50 + 5.25 = $16.25.

Step 7: If Mark didn't hire an accountant, half his weekly net income would be (7.00 + 1.50) ÷ 2 = $4.25. His parent's matching contribution on this amount would be about $6.38.

▲ The total weekly savings increase would be $7.50 + $4.25 + $6.38 = $18.13.

Candid Confectioner

▲▲▲▲▲▲▲▲▲▲▲▲▲▲▲▲▲▲▲▲▲▲▲

Facts: 1. Mileage between cities is listed in the diagram.
2. Truck gets 12 miles per gallon.
3. Gas costs $1.35 per gallon.
4. They start deliveries in Dentureville (D)
5. daily deliveries
6. 250 work days per year.

One Approach: As discussed in *Conversation Piece* in the side column, there is no short-cut to finding the best path. The following sample solution uses a diagram to show distances between towns and to trace possible routes. Trial-and-error is used to test these routes.

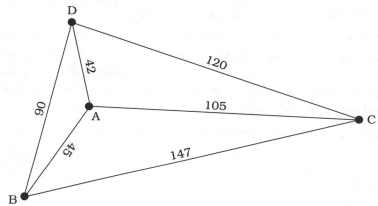

Step 1: List possible routes.

D-A-B-C-D	D-C-B-A-D
D-A-C-B-D	D-B-C-A-D
D-B-A-C-D	D-C-A-B-D

Step 2: Eliminate redundant routes. The 3 routes listed in the right column in Step 1 are just the routes in the left column reversed. Noticing this fact saves work when calculating distances.

Step 3: Calculate distances for each route.
D-A-B-C-D: 42 + 45 + 147 + 120 = 354 miles.
D-A-C-B-D: 42 + 105 + 147 + 90 = 384 miles.
D-B-A-C-D: 90 + 45 + 105 +120 = 360 miles.

▲ The shortest routes are D-A-B-C-D and D-C-B-A-D. They are each 354 miles long.

Step 4: The best routes are 30 miles shorter than the worst routes. In one year, the company can save 250 x 30 = 7500 miles.

Step 5: The company will save 7500 miles ÷ 12 miles per gallon = 625 gallons of fuel, which cost $1.35 per gallon. 625 x $1.35 = $843.75.

▲ The company can save ≈ $840 per year by finding the best route.

MORE THAN ONE APPROACH

Some students may look at the picture and make an intuitive guess about which route is shortest. Ask them to explain the reasoning behind their guesses and then to work through the problem to see if they were correct. Ask students if they can tell you why making judgments based on just the diagram might be misleading. (The lines represent routes, not roads, and the lengths of the lines aren't necessarily indicative of the driving distances.)

A GENTLE REMINDER

A calculator is a must for this type of problem. Let students focus on the idea of the problem, finding the shortest delivery route.

CONVERSATION PIECE

Trial-and-error works well for this problem, because there were only 4 towns. If there were 10 towns, there would be 181,440 possible routes. It quickly gets worse—with 20 towns, there would be about 61 quadrillion routes. (Conversation Piece in the solution on page 125 shows how to calculate the number of routes.)

Although trial-and-error will always yield the optimum solution, this approach is not practical when there are many locations to be visited. Even a computer often can't help. For example, in the 20-town problem just mentioned, a computer that calculates distances for 1 million routes per second would take 1929 years to find the shortest route.

There are no magic methods that will always yield the best possible solution quickly, but there are algorithms that will usually find a suitable solution.

Meeting Ms. Right

▲▲▲▲▲▲▲▲▲▲▲▲▲▲▲▲

Facts:
1. 800 students in school
2. Only 15% had hazel eyes.
3. 30% of hazel-eyed students were short enough.
4. 50% of those were girls.
5. 1/3 of those eliminated because they were older.
6. 3/4 eliminated because they didn't want to go.
7. Only 1 of remaining list said yes.

One Approach: As in the problem on page 61, the students do not need to know how to calculate with percents before doing this problem. The diagrams shown, drawn from the facts, are slightly different from those in the solution to problem on page 108 and illustrate how diagrams may vary.

The first diagram shows 15 students (representing 15%) taken from each 100 of the initial group. The tricky part is reasoning from the second diagram that 30 out of every 100 implies 3 out of every 10. The third diagram shows that half (50%) of the students were girls. The fourth and fifth diagrams show the remaining groups, divided into thirds and then fourths.

▲ Of the 3 girls left, 2 turned down Jordan's invitation.

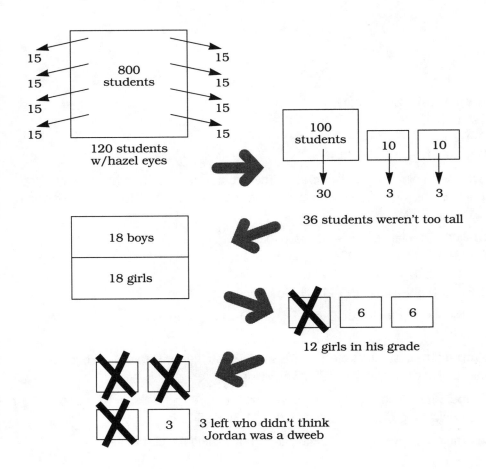

120 students w/hazel eyes

36 students weren't too tall

12 girls in his grade

3 left who didn't think Jordan was a dweeb

Maya's Early Retirement

Facts:
1. 3-step process for Gluzzies
2. cutting fabric: 10 per hour
3. sewing and stuffing: 6 per hour
4. putting on eyes and yellow fuzz: 15 per hour
5. 10 employees
6. 8-hour workday

One Approach: The goal is to distribute the employees among the 3 tasks so that the assembly line produces the maximum number of Gluzzies per hour. The production rate is determined by the step that yields the fewest finished pieces per hour. For instance, if 7 people did the last step, producing 105 Gluzzies per hour, there wouldn't be enough employees left for the first two steps to keep up with this pace.

A trial-and-error approach was used to derive the final assignment of tasks as shown in the following diagram. The starting point was to assign the most people to the slowest task, sewing and stuffing.

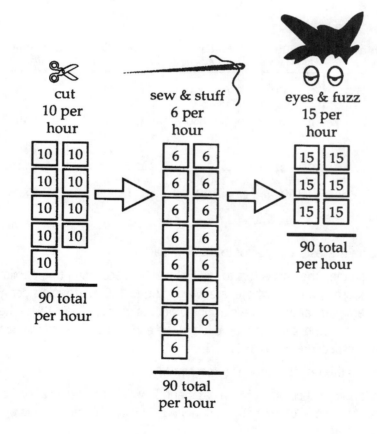

In an 8-hour day, the factory can produce 240 Gluzzies.

MORE THAN ONE APPROACH

You can provide small cards of 3 different colors to represent the 3 types of work stations. On these cards, students can write the appropriate production rates. They can then move the cards around until they find the best arrangement.

An insightful student may solve this problem in a different manner, beginning by figuring out that the 3 steps take 6, 10, and 4 minutes, respectively, for 1 Gluzzie, which is 20 minutes in all. There are 10 employees x 60 minutes = 600 employee minutes in an hour, so the maximum number of Gluzzies that can be produced in an hour is 600 ÷ 20 = 30. Enough employees would then be assigned to each step to meet this production rate.

AN EXTRA HELPING

1. What if only 8 Gluzzies could be cut out in an hour? (Real-world problems don't usually yield such "tidy" answers.)

2. How many employees should be assigned to one task if somebody stays home for the day?

3. Would it be worthwhile to hire another employee? To what task should that employee be assigned?

4. Pose Question 3, but stipulate that the new employee could divide his or her time among tasks. Ask students to describe the schedule of this employee.

Inspecting Mibzopplers

Facts: 1. 5 machines

2. Each machine makes 150 mibzopplers per hour.

3. 15 inspectors who can inspect 65, 60, 60, 55, 55, 55, 50, 50, 45, 45, 45, 45, 40, 40, 30 mibzopplers per hour.

4. Some mibzopplers are left to be inspected after 7 hours of operation.

One Approach: At first glance, it might seem that the 15 inspectors should be split evenly among the 5 machines, but it turns out that random assignment is not the best solution. For example, assigning the 3 best inspectors to one machine would waste their talents; they could inspect 185 (65 + 60 + 60) mibzopplers per hour, but the machine produces only 150 per hour. The sample solution below was based on trial-and-error and a bit of reasoning. The five machines were drawn and inspectors were assigned to one machine at a time, beginning with those inspectors who could inspect the most mibzopplers per hour.

Inspectors

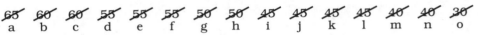

~~65~~ ~~60~~ ~~60~~ ~~55~~ ~~55~~ ~~55~~ ~~50~~ ~~50~~ ~~45~~ ~~45~~ ~~45~~ ~~45~~ ~~40~~ ~~40~~ ~~30~~
 a   b   c   d   e   f   g   h   i   j   k   l   m   n   o

machine #1	machine #2	machine #3	machine #4	machine #5
a 65	b 60	c 60	e 55	f 55
d 55	g 50	h 50	i 45	k 45
o 30	m 40	n 40	j 45	l 45
total = 150	total = 150	total = 150	total = 145	total = 145

Step 1: Assign the fastest inspector to the first machine.

Step 2: Assign the other inspectors to the first machine according to the following criteria: (1) Choose inspectors whose rate will add up to 150 mibzopplers per hour, which is the same rate at which the machine produces mibzopplers. (2) Use the fastest inspectors first, because if they're left at the end, it may be hard to choose groups whose inspecting total is 150.

Step 3: Repeat this reasoning for all 5 machines.

Step 4: Each hour, inspectors at Machines 4 and 5 will fall behind by a total of 10 mibzopplers. At the end of a 7-hour work period, 7 x 10 = 70 mibzopplers will be left to be inspected.

▲ The diagram shows the assignment of inspectors to the machines.

Games for Grades

▲▲▲▲▲▲▲▲▲▲▲▲▲▲▲▲▲▲▲

Facts: 1. Each person has 50 marbles.

2. cards: 2 jacks, 2 queens, 2 kings, 2 aces

3. 2 drawn at a time, reshuffled after each round

4. If 2 match, student puts 5 marbles into can.

5. If 2 don't match, Ms. McGill puts 1 marble into can.

One Approach: The solution shown starts with a diagram of all the possible pairs that can be drawn. From there, reasoning leads to determine who has a better chance of winning the card game: students or Ms. McGill.

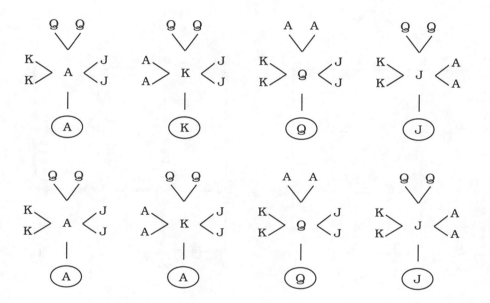

Step 1: The center letter in each of the groups above shows the 8 possible cards that can be drawn from the pack first. Surrounding each of these cards are the possibilities for the second card drawn.

Step 2: There are 56 possible pairs that can be drawn. The ones in which both cards match (and the student wins) are circled. There are only 8 possibilities out of 56 in which the student wins the round.

Step 3: There are 48 possibilities out of 56 for Ms. McGill to win the round. She should win 48 ÷ 8 = 6 times as many rounds as the student player. This more than compensates for the fact that when a student wins the round, he or she puts in 5 times as many marbles as Ms. McGill.

▲ Over the course of a 50-marble game, Ms. McGill has a slight edge over the students. Students with low grades might still see the game as being worthwhile. However, the student in the problem got a B on the test; he or she may not want to take the chance since the odds are in the teacher's favor.

MORE THAN ONE APPROACH

This problem may seem formidable to many students before they begin solving it. However, it unfolds nicely after the first steps are taken. Some students may need help just understanding the game. Give them some cards and let them try it. All sorts of items can be substituted for the marbles in the can; students can even keep track of the rounds won with a pencil and paper.

Other students will do well if you give them a set of 8 cards like the set used for the game and ask them to show you all the possible pairs that can be drawn. As their understanding of the game and the possible outcomes develops, lead them toward expressing these ideas in a diagram.

Some students may see the symmetry in the possible outcomes. In the upper left grouping in the diagram, there is 1 chance for the student and 6 chances for Ms. McGill to win. These odds are duplicated in every other grouping in the diagram.

A GENTLE REMINDER

Encourage students to act out problems; it often helps them to see and understand what's going on. For Games for Grades, acting out the problem means playing the game or using cards to discover the possible pairs, as described above in More Than One Approach.

The Pedaling Editor

MORE THAN ONE APPROACH

Students will probably use trial-and-error, although some may mix trial-and-error with reasoning. Give students the opportunity to share their reasoning by allowing them to work in small groups. Then discuss the problem as a class.

A GENTLE REMINDER

Although you should always give students a chance to try out their own methods before showing short-cuts, they will often enjoy hearing about clever techniques, such as dynamic programming. However, be careful not to be so anxious to share your inside information that you overlook opportunities to praise students' ideas. After students solve Julie the Pedaling Editor, share the dynamic programming approach as an interesting technique, not as the solution you wanted them to use.

AN EXTRA HELPING

Ask students to tell you how many possible routes there are from A to B (traveling north and east only). The diagram below shows a way to solve this problem. There is only one route from A to J and one route from A to N. Next, K can be reached from J or from N, so there are two routes from A to K. Work towards B, determining the number of routes from A to each intersection as you go.

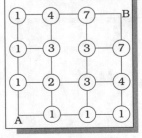

Facts: 1. The distances between intersections are shown (in yards) in the diagram on the left below. Julie wants to find the shortest route from A to B.

One Approach: This sample solution is based on an approach called dynamic programming, which is used to solve certain optimization problems. You should not expect students to use this method to solve the problem; this sophisticated approach is presented because it's so elegant. However, in their trial-and-error approaches to this problem, students may use at least part of the reasoning inherent in the dynamic programming approach. Please read *A Gentle Reminder* before sharing this solution with students.

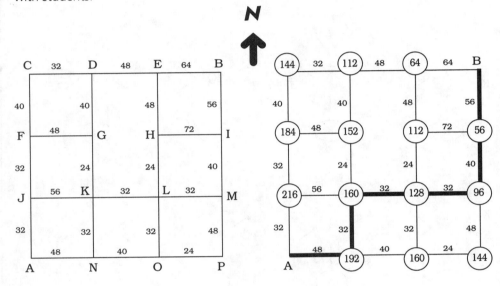

Step 1: Assume that Julie will travel only north or east; traveling south or west would take her in the wrong direction. Refer to the diagrams above.

Step 2: Begin at B and work backwards. The shortest (and only) route from E to B is 64 yards long. Similarly, the shortest route from D to B is 112 yards long, and the shortest route from C to B is 144 yards long.

Step 3: Using the same logic as in Step 2, determine the shortest routes from I, M, and P to B. These are shown in the diagram.

Step 4: There are two options from point H: Julie could travel north to E and then east to B, or she could go east to I and then north to B. These options are 112 and 112 yards long, respectively. The first option is shorter, and the minimum distance of 112 yards is labeled at point H in the diagram on the right.

Step 5: Work backwards towards A, labeling the minimum distance from each intersection as you go.

▲ The minimum travel distance for Julie is along the path A-N-K-L-M-I-B (bold-faced in the diagram). It is 240 yards long.

Trent's Tongue Tricks

▲▲▲▲▲▲▲▲▲▲▲▲▲▲▲▲▲▲▲▲▲

Facts: 1. 200 students
2. 15% could say tongue twister.
3. 45% could curl their tongues.
4. overlap: 5% could do both

One Approach: This problem can be solved in many ways. This sample solution shows how a student who doesn't know how to use Venn diagrams might solve the problem.

Step 1: Change the percents into numbers of people. Students can do this by calculating or using diagrams.

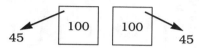

The diagram shows that 45% taken out of 200 people is equal to 90 people. There are 90 tongue curlers.

Step 2: Following the procedure in Step 1, you can determine that there are 30 people who can say the tongue twister and 10 people who can curl their tongues *and* say the tongue twister.

Step 3: The diagram below shows the people in the group who can do at least one tongue trick. The people who can do neither are not shown. The difficult part of this problem is accounting for those people who can do both tongue tricks. The diagram below handles this difficulty by representing them with a circle *and* a square.

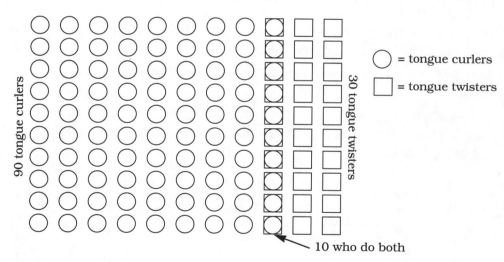

○ = tongue curlers

□ = tongue twisters

10 who do both

Step 4: The diagram shows 110 people. There must be 200 - 110 = 90 people who can't do either trick.

Step 5: Reason that 90 people out of 200 is equivalent to 45 people out of 100, so 45% of the people can't do either trick.

▲ There are 90 people who can do neither skill, which is 45% of the group.

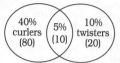

MORE THAN ONE APPROACH

Students could use a Venn diagram like the one below:

40% curlers (80)   5% (10)   10% twisters (20)

The percents could be used directly to conclude that, since 55% of the students are in the circles, 45% must be outside of the circles. The next logical step would be to calculate that 45% of 200 is 90, so there are 90 students.

Students may make two common errors that both have to do with mishandling the 5% overlap between the two skill groups. Counting this 5% as a separate group will lead to the conclusion that 35% of the students can do neither skill. However, students may also reason incorrectly that the 5% should be subtracted from both the 45% tongue-curling group and the 15% tongue-twisting group. Calculations based on this assumption will show that 50% of the students are in this group.

LEADING QUESTIONS

"I love your diagram, but there's one thing I think you may be overlooking. Look at Fact 4. Tell me what the word overlap means."

AN EXTRA HELPING

Add a third tongue twister and specify the percentage of students who can say it. Also specify the percentage of students who have each combination of two skills and the percentage with all three skills. A 3-circle Venn diagram will help to solve this problem.

A Lion and His Socks

Facts:
1. 4 red socks in drawer
2. 4 green socks in drawer
3. Pull out 2 at a time.
4. Try each day for a year (365 days)

One Approach: Although there are some shortcuts, as discussed in *More Than One Approach*, the following solution is based on a diagram that shows every possible combination to pull out a pair of socks.

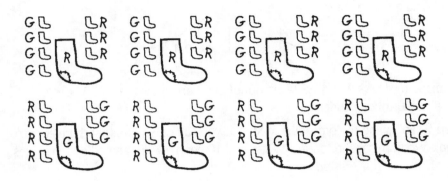

Step 1: The large socks in the diagram above show the 8 possible first socks that could be pulled from the drawer. The smaller socks around each large sock show the possible second socks. It is apparent that the socks will be mismatched more often than they'll match.

Step 2: Count the combinations. There are 8 x 7 = 56 possible pairs. Out of these pairs, there are 8 x 4 = 32 that don't match.

Step 3: Out of every 56 draws, mismatched socks should be pulled out about 32 times.

Step 4: Divide the year into 56-day segments. The 29 days left at the end make close to a half a segment, so only 32 ÷ 2 = 16 mismatched pairs should be pulled out during these days.

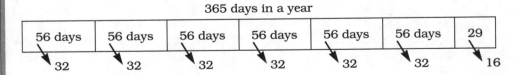

365 days in a year

56 days	56 days	56 days	56 days	56 days	56 days	29
32	32	32	32	32	32	16

Out of every 56 days, socks that don't match should be pulled out 32 times.

Step 5: Add up the total number of days for mismatched socks. (32 x 6) + 16 = 208.

▲ Socks that don't match should be pulled approximately 208 out of the 365 days in the year.

MORE THAN ONE APPROACH

Students may discover several short-cuts. First, they may notice that no matter which sock is taken out first, there are 4 choices in 7 of then taking out a sock of the opposite color. Note that 4/7 is equivalent to 32/56, which is the ratio found in the sample solution.

Some students may also notice that 7 is the number of days in a week, so socks should be mismatched on about 4 days of every week. Through 52 weeks, 4 x 52 = 208 pairs of mismatched socks should be pulled out.

If students are having trouble discovering and listing the combinations, give them small strips of red and green paper and ask them to act out the possibilities.

A GENTLE REMINDER

Students will eagerly approach you to find out if their answers are correct. Don't tell them. Instead, ask them to show you what they've done. As they explain their reasoning, let them know what you like about their thinking, listing of the facts, careful work, diagrams, and unique ideas. When they've finished, encourage them to make a statement about their work and their answer.

AN EXTRA HELPING

1. What are the chances of pulling out 3 socks in a row that are all of the same color?

2. If there are also 4 orange socks in the drawer, what are the chances of drawing the different possible pairs?

See What I Saw

▲▲▲▲▲▲▲▲▲▲▲▲▲▲▲▲

Facts:
1. Bigfoot weighs 868 lbs.
2. Narrator weighs 124 lbs.
3. Seesaw is 12' long.
4. Bigfoot and narrator on ends of seesaw.

One Approach: Solving this problem requires inductive reasoning based on the seesaw example in the problem. The weight on the right was twice the weight on the left, so the length of the seesaw on the left had to be twice the length of the seesaw on the right. This relationship can be expressed algebraically (as shown below), but students don't know algebra. Instead, they must use reasoning to locate the fulcrum to balalnce the narrator and Bigfoot.

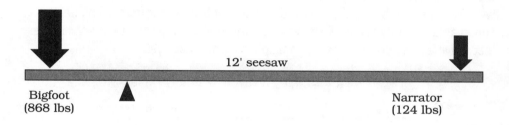

12' seesaw

Bigfoot
(868 lbs)

Narrator
(124 lbs)

Step 1: Bigfoot's side weighs 868 ÷ 124 = 7 times the narrator's side.

Step 2: Using inductive reasoning from the example, the distance on the right of the fulcrum must be 7 times the distance on the left side.

Step 3: The seesaw is 12 ft long. Using trial-and-error, suppose that the distance on the left was 2'; then the distance on the right would be 2' x 7 = 14' This would make 16' altogether, which is too long. Similarly, 1' on the left and 7' on the right only add up to 8', which is too short. Continue with this approach to get distances that work.

▲ The fulcrum should be 1.5' away from Bigfoot and 10.5' away from the narrator.

In the diagram below, the distances from the two ends of the seesaw to the fulcrum are labeled d_1 and d_2. The weights on either end are labeled W_1 and W_2. In order for the seesaw (or lever) to be balanced, the equation shown below the diagram must be true. The distances and the weights are inversely related; as one goes up, the other must go down. This equation can be extended to describe a lever with many weights. The sum of the weight-distance products on both sides of the fulcrum must be equal.

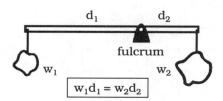

$$w_1 d_1 = w_2 d_2$$

A GENTLE REMINDER

Is there a conference area in your room where a pair of students can discuss a problem? Like their adult counterparts solving problems at their jobs, students often need to share ideas in order to move ahead. As discussed in Learning Styles & Individual Tastes in Chapter 2, many students think better if they're talking about their thoughts to another person.

Begin the year by modeling how to use conferences to share ideas without giving answers. Also, clearly state your expectations for the use of the conference area(s), keeping in mind that paired sharing should not disturb those students who need a quiet area to work.

AN EXTRA HELPING

1. How much weight would Bigfoot have to lose so that the fulcrum could be moved 1/2' closer to the narrator? (248 lbs.)

2. Suppose the fulcrum were placed in the middle of the seesaw and Littlefoot joined the narrator on the right side. If Littlefoot weighs 372 lbs, where should he stand so the seesaw is balanced? (3' from the fulcrum)

3. Try making up your own seesaw problems.

Planetary Health Crisis

Facts:
1. One person is infected with billow virus.
2. First person spreads virus to 2 others each year.
3. Each person with virus spreads it to 2 others each year.
4. 10-year period of spread

One Approach: The facts, the diagram, and the sample solution are for the second case described, in which every person with the virus spreads it to two others each year. (Refer to the solution on page 109 for an explanation of the scenario in which each Purlonian infected spreads it to only one other Purlonian during each time period. At the end of 10 years, 1024 Purlonians will be affected.)

In this solution, Purlonians were added to the diagram until a pattern could be seen. The number of Purlonians with the virus each year was three times the number from the previous year. This information was used to fill in the rest of the chart on the left. The chart on the right, showing the spread of billow virus from each infected Purlonian to five others each year, was made by inferring from the two simpler cases that the infected population would multiply itself by 5 each year.

1st person — end of 1st year
— end of 2nd year
— end of 3rd year

Each Purlonian Spreads Virus to 2 Others Each Year		Each Purlonian Spreads Virus to 5 Others Each Year	
year	with virus	year	with virus
1	3	1	5
2	9	2	25
3	27	3	125
4	81	4	625
5	243	5	3125
6	729	6	15,625
7	2187	7	78,125
8	6561	8	390,625
9	19,683	9	1,953,125
10	59,049	10	9,765,625

Flying Zorks of Migork

▲▲▲▲▲▲▲▲▲▲▲▲▲▲▲▲▲▲▲▲▲▲▲

Facts: 1. 4-machine assembly line, 14 machines in all
2. products per hour: meznorter (22), grank (16), haftep (13), blemp (7)

One Approach: This solution is based on trial-and-error and reasoning.

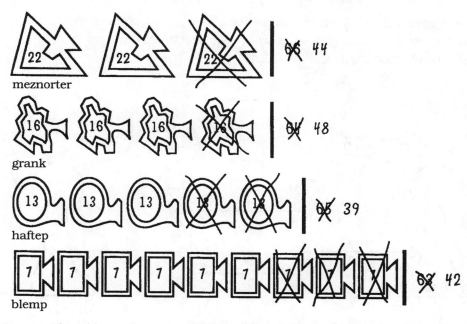

meznorter

grank

haftep

blemp

MORE THAN ONE APPROACH

Some students may develop a system for adding machines to the factory. Here is a system that works: (1) Start with one machine of each type. (2) Add a blemp, which currently has the slowest production rate. (3) Now blemps complete 14 products per hour, but hafteps complete only 13, so add a haftep. (4) Continue in this manner, always adding a machine of the type that currently has the slowest production rate. Stop when there are 14 machines.

CONVERSATION PIECE

Here's an unusual solution:
1. First, review the solution on page 117 to see how the number of products completed turned out to be a common multiple of the production rates of the 3 steps.
2. A common multiple of the Smipsmace machine rates is 22 x 16 x 13 x 7 = 32,032.
3. It would take 1456, 2002, 2464, and 4576 of the four machine types to produce 32,032 products per hour.
4. This HUGE factory (with 10,498 machines) is ≈ 750 times bigger than a 14-machine factory.
5. Divide the number of machines in Step 3 by 750 to get 1.9 meznorters, 2.7 granks, 3.3 hafteps, and 6.1 blemps. Compare these numbers to the sample solution.

Step 1: There have to be more of the slower machines so they can keep up with the production rate set by the faster machines.

Step 2: Start with 3 meznorters (the fastest machine). The meznorter completes 22 ÷ 7 = 3 times as many Smipsmaces per hour as the blemp (the slowest machine). If there are 3 meznorters, there should be 9 blemps.

Step 3: Both the grank and the haftep are about twice as fast as the blemp. Consequently, the 9 blemps have been matched in speed with 4 granks and 5 hafteps. The production rates for these machines are shown in the diagram. (They are the crossed-out values.)

Step 4: There are now 3 + 4 + 5 + 9 = 21 machines, which is 7 too many.

Step 5: Remove 1 meznorter (crossed out in the diagram). Following the reasoning of Steps 2 and 3, remove 3 blemps, 2 hafteps, and one grank. There are now 14 machines. Adjust the production rates.

Step 6: The hafteps complete the fewest Smipsmaces. If a blemp is given up to add a haftep, the hafteps will complete 13 x 4 = 52 products per hour, but the blemps will be able to complete only 7 x 5 = 35 products per hour. This rate is worse than the 39 products per hour produced by the 3 hafteps shown. Changing meznorters or granks into hafteps would lower the rate even more. The production rates of the four steps are now as balanced as they can be.

▲ The factory can produce 39 Smipsmaces per hour.

Czech Mate

▲▲▲▲▲▲▲▲▲▲▲▲

Facts:
1. Jarda earns $120 each month.
2. He bets 15% on chess w/ Dad & 10% on chess w/ Mom.
3. Mom wins 3/5 of games, but Dad only wins 1/5 of games.
4. 30% for spending money/25% for expenses

One Approach: This sample solution assumes that students know how to find a specified percent of a number, either by calculation or by reasoning similar to the first demonstration problem of this chapter.

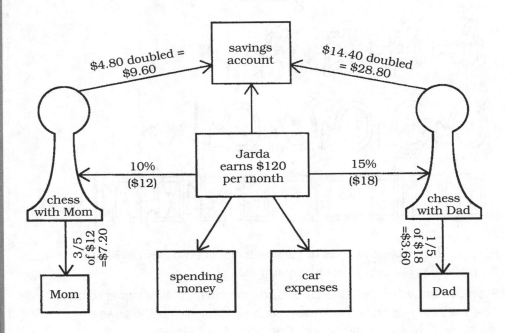

Step 1: Use the facts to build a diagram. Translate percents into dollars.

Step 2: Handling the chess money is tricky. Dad gets 1/5 (or $3.60) of the $18.00 Jarda bets with him. The remaining $14.40 goes into Jarda's savings account, along with another $14.40 from his dad to pay on the bets he lost. Similarly, 2 x $4.80 = $9.60 goes into Jarda's savings account from the chess games with his mom.

Step 3: Only 70% of Jarda's income is accounted for, so the other 30% (or $36.00) must go to his savings account. A total of $38.40 goes into the savings account from chess games. This amount accounts for 100 x ($38.40)/($36.00 + $38.40) ≈ 52% of the monthly savings.

Step 4: Jarda <u>could</u> put the $30.00 he bets on chess directly into this savings account, but by playing chess he gets an extra $38.40 - $30.00 = $8.40.

▲ About 52% of Jarda's savings come from chess games. By playing chess, Jarda makes a monthly profit of $8.40.

Drilling for Dollars

▲▲▲▲▲▲▲▲▲▲▲▲▲▲▲▲▲▲▲▲▲▲▲

Facts: 1. Drill follows path ABCEDA.
2. reduce distance of drill path by at least 10%
3. Distances shown in diagram.

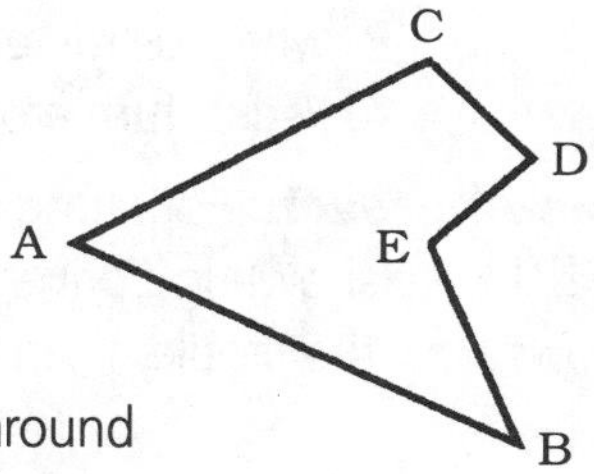

One Approach: Although trial-and-error was used for this sample solution, reasoning can also be used to make "best guesses." For example, path ACBEDA crosses back and forth through the middle of the area enclosed by the holes. It seems more likely that a path around the perimeter, such as ACDEBA, would be shorter. The data in the table below shows this to be the case.

The 10 paths listed in the table are the only possible routes. (See below.) Each path can be reversed to generate a different order in the holes, but the lengths of these reversed paths will be the same as the length of the paths listed.

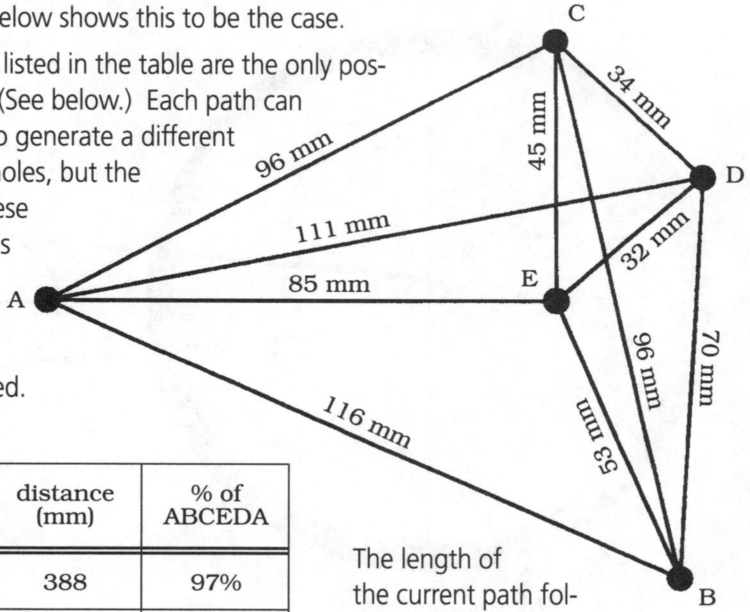

path	distance (mm)	% of ABCEDA
ACBEDA	388	97%
ACBDEA	379	95%
ACEDBA	359	90%
ACEBDA	375	94%
ACDEBA	331	83%
ACDBEA	338	85%
ABCEDA	400	100%
ABCDEA	363	91%
ABECDA	359	90%
ABDCEA	350	88%
AEBCDA	379	95%
AECBDA	407	102%

The length of the current path followed by the drill is 400 mm long. This distance has to be reduced by 10% (or 40 mm). The middle column shows that five paths are each less than or equal to the 360 mm required. Each of these paths reversed would also be short enough.

The right hand column shows each path's distance as a percentage of the original path's distance. The three shortest paths all go around the perimeter of the group of holes. However, it is possible for there to be a configuration in which the shortest path involves criss-crossing through the center.

Diagram labels: C, D, A, E, B

Distances: 96 mm, 34 mm, 45 mm, 111 mm, 85 mm, 32 mm, 116 mm, 96 mm, 70 mm, 53 mm

MORE THAN ONE APPROACH

1. Refer to the information given with the solution on page 113.

2. Expect some students to develop strategies for choosing a path. One strategy is to visit the closest unvisited location until all locations have been visited. Give students ample time to share their ideas while they work on the problem.

CONVERSATION PIECE

If N locations are to be visited, we can write an equation to describe the number of routes that need to be considered.

1. From the starting point, there are (N-1) locations that could be visited first.

2. From each of these (N-1) points, there are (N-2) points that could be visited second. Consequently, there are (N-1) x (N-2) possible routes for the first 2 legs of the journey.

3. At each location visited, the number of options is 1 less than the number of options at the previous location. The total number of possible routes is: (N-1) x (N-2) x (N-3)...... x 1

4. This product can be written as (N-1)!. As mentioned in the sample solution, half of the paths are just the reverse of the other half. Therefore, the number of solutions that need to be considered is (N-1)!/2.

5. For the problem shown, N=5, so (N-1)!/2 = 4!/2 = (4 x 3 x 2 x 1)/2 = 12.

Speeds & Sprockets

Facts:
1. front sprocket diameter: 6″
2. back sprocket diameters: 1st gear-4″, 2nd gear-3″, 3rd gear-2″
3. wheel diameter: 25″
4. Pedals turn around once.

One Approach: Equations for analyzing the motion of gears or wheels connected by belts are shown in *Conversation Piece* to the left. However, the sample solution shows how the problem can be solved with a knowledge of circles only.

CONVERSATION PIECE

The diagram below shows two wheels connected by a belt or chain. Under the diagram are the variables that describe the wheels' diameters, angular displacements, and angular velocities. The following equations show how these variables are related. (These equations also apply to gears that turn one another.)

$$\frac{d_1}{d_2} = \frac{T_2}{T_1} \ \text{ and } \ \frac{d_1}{d_2} = \frac{N_2}{N_1}$$

In other words, both the angular displacement and the velocity of the two wheels vary inversely with their diameters; the smaller the wheel, the faster it will turn. That's why the bike travels faster in 3rd gear than in 1st gear: the 3rd-gear sprocket is smaller than the 1st-gear sprocket. However, there is a trade-off. A small wheel takes a stronger twist (or torque) to turn it. It's hard to pedal in 3rd gear when you first start out. The larger sprocket (1st gear) is used to keep the bicycle moving at a higher velocity.

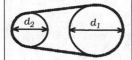

WHEEL #1

d_1=diameter
T_1=number of turns
N_1= turns per second

WHEEL #2

d_2=diameter
T_2=number of turns
N_2= turns per second

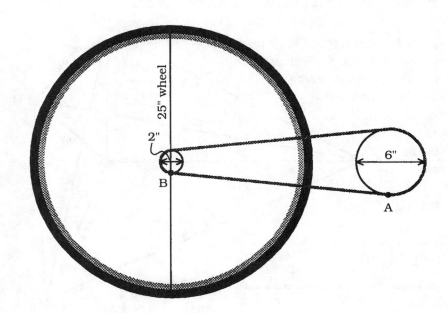

Step 1: Recall that the circumference of a circle equals π (≈3.14) times its diameter.

Step 2: When the 6″ sprocket turns around once, Point A on the chain will move a distance equal to the circumference of the sprocket, which is equal to π x diameter = π x 6 ≈ 18.85″.

Step 3: Point B on the small sprocket will move the same distance as Point A. Also, the circumference of the 2″ sprocket is π x 2. To find out how many circumferences of the 2″ sprocket will be traveled by Point B, divide the distance that B will travel by the length of a single circumference. 18.85 ÷ (π x 2) = 3 circumferences.

Step 4: The back wheel is attached to the small sprocket, so it will turn the same number of times as the sprocket. If the back wheel turns 3 times, then it will travel 3 of its circumferences along the road. This distance is $3 \times \pi \times 25 \approx 236''$.

▲ The values for each combination are shown in the table.

gear	back sprocket diameter	# of turns	bike's movement
1st	4"	15	≈118"
2nd	3"	2	≈157"
3rd	2"	3	≈236"

Kaely's CAT Dreams

Facts:
1. There are 9 patients to be scheduled.
2. 2 CAT scanners are available.
3. This diagram shows the times and priorities for each patient.

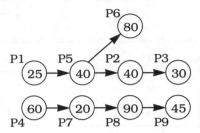

One Approach: The quality of a solution depends on more than just numbers; it depends on balancing the needs of individual doctors and patients with the needs of the entire hospital. Two options are described below. The goal is to have the students experiment with techniques and possible schedules and then discuss the advantages and disadvantages of each proposed plan.

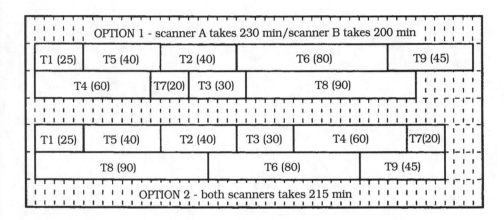

Both schedules are drawn on grid paper, where each rectangle represents 5 minutes. The T's stand for tasks to be completed, and the time required for each task is shown in parentheses.

OPTION 1: The indicated priorities of the patients was the controlling factor in generating this schedule. Whenever a scanner was available, the uncompleted task with the highest priority was assigned to it. Tasks 2 and 3 came later in the schedule because they couldn't be completed until after Tasks 1 and 5.

OPTION 2: To generate this schedule, an attempt was made to equalize the total time used by the two scanners. Altogether, the nine tasks take 430 minutes. Task combinations totaling 215 minutes were assigned to each machine, with scheduling according to priorities wherever possible. The advantage of this schedule is that it takes less time to finish the tasks. However, the order in which the tasks are completed may not be acceptable to the physicians who requested them.

MORE THAN ONE APPROACH

Graph paper is very handy for speeding up the time it takes to draw schedules. You may want to tell students that it's available if they want to use it without telling them how to use it. Let them discover techniques on their own.

Another technique that students may discover is to make scaled rectangles representing the tasks and then to move them around to build a variety of schedules. You can share either of these techniques with students after they have had a chance to think of ideas on their own.

A GENTLE REMINDER

Problem solving is an approach to math. Look for other problem-solving techniques that you can share with students. Use problems in this book as a model for creating your own problems for each math topic you teach. Nurture and evaluate the process by which your students solve problems, and encourage diversity in their solutions.

AN EXTRA HELPING

Have the students work in pairs or groups of three. Ask each group to choose a schedule for the scanners that they think is the best. Ask "What if?" questions such as, "What if Task 5 took 60 minutes instead of 40?" The groups should respond by analyzing and commenting on how these unforeseen changes change their schedules. You can even assign dollar values for the time the scanners are in use and then ask groups to tell you how much the unexpected schedule changes would cost the hospital.

Toothpaste in the Basement

Facts:
1. 4 ingredients
2. Tank #1: Candy Madness
   - 1 gal of A, 2 gal of B, and 3 gal of D
   - 1/3 is pumped into Maple Sugar Supreme tank.
   - 2/3 is drained and packaged.
3. Tank #2: Maple Sugar Supreme
   - 3 times the amount of A used in Candy Madness
   - 2 gal of C for every 3 gal of A
   - 21 gal are produced every hour.

One Approach: The sample solution is based on reasoning that has the flavor of algebra but doesn't require formal algebraic operations.

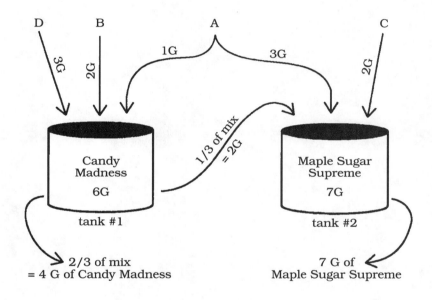

Step 1: Label the flow of ingredient A into Tank 1, with 1G to stand for each gallon of liquid being pumped.

Step 2: Draw and label all the other flows into Tank 1 according to the facts. Relate each one to the 1G flow of ingredient A. For example, 2 gallons of C for every 1 gallon of A are pumped into Tank 1, so this flow should be labeled 2G.

Step 3: When A, B, and D are mixed in Tank 1, it makes 6G of toothpaste. One third of this amount, or 2G, is pumped into Tank 2.

Step 4: Draw and label the flows into Tank 2. A total of 2G + 3G + 2G = 7G accumulating every hour.

MORE THAN ONE APPROACH
Starting with a letter to represent the flow of A into tank 1 is actually a very clever technique for students to use. Instead, students might just label this flow as 1 gallon per hour and then relate the rest of the flows to this value, as in the sample solution. When the last step is reached, these students will have to reckon with the difference between the 7 gallons in tank 2 and the 21 gallons that come out of tank 2. Perhaps they will see that every quantity needs to be multiplied by 3. If they follow this reasoning, have them go back through the facts to make sure the new values all make sense.

A GENTLE REMINDER
Be aware of tools your students do or do not have at their disposal. In solving Toothpaste in the Basement, students don't know algebra. Be careful not to lead students into an approach that is really yours, not theirs.

LEADING QUESTIONS
"You're stuck? But your arrows all look excellent. Okay, why don't you just pretend for now that this flow of A into Tank 1 is 1 gallon per hour. What would this flow of B be equal to? Good. How about C? Good. Keep going and see what happens."

Step 5: The 7G of Maple Sugar Supreme makes up 21 gallons, so 1G is actually   21 ÷ 7 = 3 gallons.

Step 6: Two-thirds, or 4G, of the Candy Madness is drained and packaged every hour. 4G is equal to 4 x 3 = 12 gallons per hour.

▲ Elana's process produces 12 gallons of Candy Madness per hour.

ANNOTATED
Bibliography

Personality Types and Learning Styles

Lawrence, Gordon. *People Types and Tiger Stripes: A Practical Guide to Learning Styles.* Center for Applications of Psychological Type, 1979.

> Describes the application of Myers-Briggs Type information to the classroom. Helps teachers identify students' learning styles, and suggests methods of planning instruction to help students make the most of their assets.

Myers, Isabel Briggs. *Gifts Differing.* Consulting Psychologist Press, Inc. 1980.

> Isabel Briggs-Myers co-authored the Myers-Briggs Type Indicator with Katherine Briggs. Her book presents both narrative and statistical information describing the theories behind her work on personality types.

Williams, Linda Verlee. *Teaching for the Two-Sided Mind.* Simon & Schuster, Inc. 1986.

> Describes the functioning of the brain's left and right hemispheres, and provides teaching strategies that enable students to use both sides of their brains.

Philosophies and Techniques of Math Instruction

Charles Randall, Frank Lester, and Phares O'Daffer. *How to Evaluate Progress in Problem Solving.* NCTM, 1987.

> Describes a variety of techniques for assessing students' problem-solving work. Techniques include observing, questioning, holistic scoring, interviewing, and students' self-assessment.

National Council of Teachers of Mathematics (NCTM). *Curriculum and Evaluation Standards for School Mathematics*. NCTM, 1989.
> Describes a vision of what a mathematics classroom can and should be, and establishes a framework for building such a classroom. Lists specific objectives for every level.

NCTM. *Addenda Series*. NCTM, 1992.
> This series of books further delineates the ideas of the *Curriculum and Evaluation Standards*. Example activities are used to illustrate how each math objective can be met in the classroom.

Sources of Ideas

Macaulay, David. *The Way Things Work*. Houghton Mifflin Co., 1988.
> Uses fun drawings and clever narratives to explain how machines, household appliances, and vehicles work. This is an indispensable source of quick information about what mathematics, physics, and chemistry have to do with the things around us in our everyday lives.

Malkevitch, Joseph, et.al. *For All Practical Purposes: Introduction to Contemporary Mathematics*. W.H. Freeman and Company, 1988.
> Discusses applications of mathematics to scheduling, planning, voting, and making decisions.

Paulos, John Allen. *Innumeracy: Mathematical Illiteracy and Its Consequences*. Vintage Books, 1990.
> Discusses how we are led astray by our lack of number sense. Includes many interesting stories and situations that you can use as the basis for projects, problems, and discussions to be shared with your students.

Video

Futures, Produced by the Foundation for the Advancement in Science Education (FASE), 1991.

> This series of 15-minute shows, hosted by Jaime Escalante, portrays various professionals using math in their jobs. The series, and its successor (*Futures II*) is shown on educational television. It is distributed by: PBS Video, 1320 Braddock Place, Alexandria, VA, 22314.

Math Who Needs It?, Produced by FASE, 1991.

> This one-hour video features professionals at work, comedians, and celebrities, all talking about their experiences of learning math and using it in the real world. Many public television networks air this production in the fall. It is distributed by: Math, Who Needs It?/Futures, P.O. Box 847, Los Angeles, CA, 90078.